GARLAND STUDIES ON

INDUSTRIAL PRODUCTIVITY

edited by

STUART BRUCHEY
UNIVERSITY OF MAINE

A GARLAND SERIES

OCAW Local 7-515 president, Connie Malloy, at microphone, and union steward, Phyllis Fields, demonstrate with other Local 7-515 members at American Home Products Corporation headquarters in New York City in July 1992.

EXPOSING FEDERAL SPONSORSHIP OF JOB LOSS

The Whitehall Plant Closing Campaign and "Runaway Plant" Reform

JULIA C. ABEDIAN

GARLAND PUBLISHING, Inc.
NEW YORK & LONDON / 1995

Library of Congress Cataloging-in-Publication Data

Abedian, Julia C., 1960–
    Exposing federal sponsorship of job loss : the Whitehall plant
closing campaign and "runaway plant" reform /Julia C. Abedian.
        p.   cm. — (Garland studies on industrial productivity)
    Includes bibliographical references and index.
    ISBN 0-8153-1778-6 (alk. paper)
    1. Plant shutdowns—Indiana—Elkhart. 2. Pharmaceutical
industry—Indiana—Elkhart—Employees. 3. Trade-unions—
Pharmaceutical industry employees—Indiana—Elkhart.
4. Whitehall Laboratories. 5. Industrial policy—United States.
6. Corporations—Taxation—United States. 7. Corporations—
Taxation—Puerto Rico. I. Title. II. Series.
HD5708.55.U62E453 1995
338.6'042—dc20

                                                        95-37868

Printed on acid-free, 250-year-life paper
Manufactured in the United States of America

To Saip, Alexander, and Andre

Contents

Foreword

In her study of the closing of the Whitehall plant of American Home Products (AHP), Julia Abedian explores a number of subjects with great significance for labor and economic policy, especially the role of U.S. tax policy in the relocation of jobs from the continental United States to Puerto Rico. Her work demonstrates the problems for the United States because of inadequate adjustment policies to protect the interests of communities and workers when plants close and production is relocated. The almost unrestricted right of companies to make such decisions is justified at least in part by the belief that economic efficiency is advanced by giving managers almost unrestricted freedom to respond to market forces. Julia Abedian's study demonstrates, however, that these decisions are not dictated entirely by market forces, but are strongly influenced by U.S. tax, political, and foreign development policies. Almost as an afterthought, most tax and foreign development laws (like Section 936 of the tax code, which she analyzes very thoroughly) usually have provisions which ostensibly protect workers by prohibiting companies from using the federal subsidies provided by such laws to shift jobs from one place to another. Unfortunately, worker-protection provisions are rarely enforced, partly because business or political interests almost always take priority over those of displaced workers and communities. The myth is that markets will take care of workers and communities, but basic economics demonstrates that market forces are very important, but are not concerned with equity or environmental and worker protections. Indeed, under free market conditions, rational employers will shift the costs of change to workers and communities. It is for these reasons that most other democratic industrialized countries have positive adjustment programs to provide for an equitable sharing of the benefits and costs of change. In the 1950s and '60s, when the higher growth of productivity and output and relatively full employment enabled displaced workers to be readily absorbed into new jobs, costly policies like Section 936 caused less damage than they did in the 1980s and '90s, when joblessness is much higher, productivity growth is stagnant, and the globalization of production makes it easy for companies like American Home Products to shift jobs from even profitable plants to lower wage places like Puerto Rico.

It is hard to see the rationality of the subsidies provided by Section 936, which averaged $58,000 per job that paid an average of $16,000. Instead of these tax advantages, it would make more sense to have a human-resource-oriented development strategy for Puerto Rico and permit development to take place in response to competitive advantages resulting from higher productivity. It also would make sense to have an adjustment program for displaced workers which would require companies to provide economic justification for plant closings and to internalize the costs to workers and communities from plant closings to the firms that benefit from these actions.

Julia Abedian's study demonstrates that while individual unions like the Oil, Chemical, and Atomic Workers (OCAW) are powerless to prevent plant closings, there are things they can do to expose public and corporate policies that subsidize, or encourage the export of, American jobs. In this case, the OCAW was aided by some fortuitous circumstances, especially internal political processes in Puerto Rico and the United States, which made it possible to effectively focus moral condemnation on Section 936 and AHP. However, the positive outcome in this case—which made bad outcomes for AHP workers a little better—were because of the willingness of local and national union leaders to find legal, legislative, and public relations means to force AHP to compensate workers for the Elkhart, Indiana plant closing and the relocation of work to Puerto Rico with U.S. and commonwealth subsidies. The union's use of public condemnation as a tactic was effective in this case partly because AHP had nurtured a reputation as an ethical company with good labor-management relations. In addition, the high visibility of the company's products made it vulnerable to the OCAW's public relations campaign. The OCAW's campaign also was successful partly because it was able to translate a particular problem into one of general interest to workers and the public. Greater use of such tactics by other unions might strengthen business support for more effective worker and community adjustment programs.

Julia Abedian thoroughly documents the Whitehall plant closing case and analyzes the political and economic context which caused that case to be instructive for broader labor and economic policy purposes.

Ray Marshall
June 21, 1995

Preface

In 1990, I believed unions were anachronistic relics that had outlived their usefulness. During the 1980's, I had watched from a distance as my hometown, Flint, Michigan, was ravaged by the pullout of General Motors and concluded then that when a company decides to move, its workers (unionized or not) have no choice but to accept it. What other conclusion made sense when one of the country's most "powerful" unions, the United Auto Workers, seemed to have no recourse, no meaningful response, to the massive shift of jobs out of Michigan?

In the late 1980's, the company where I worked in northern Indiana dismantled itself under the debt burden of a leveraged buyout and again the union could not respond. This anecdotal evidence of the apparent powerlessness of labor was borne out *en masse* as "corporate restructuring" left hundreds of thousands of people across the country without work and unions in serious decline. Capital had all the power and that seemed to be the natural and inevitable order of the American economy. There appeared to be no alternative.

When the Oil, Chemical, and Atomic Workers Union (OCAW) began its fight with American Home Products Corporation (AHP) to prevent the closing of AHP's subsidiary Whitehall Laboratories in Elkhart, Indiana, it seemed only a matter of time before the inevitable succession of news accounts about picket lines, rallies, worker outrage, and finally, resignation to the necessity of retraining for jobs in the evolving "service" economy. Instead, arcane acronyms began to appear in the headlines: Section 936, NLRB, WARN, RICO, JTPA, and they persisted for three years. Apparently, this was a different kind of union fight.

OCAW filed lawsuits, introduced bills in Congress, participated in Congressional hearings, and appeared on national news programs in its fight to prevent the closure of Whitehall. To labor lawyers and scholars, these acronyms and legal actions undoubtedly had meaning and probably spelled out just what the union was up to. To me, they meant only one thing—here was a situation where labor

xiii

seemed smart and relevant and empowered even as it faced the direst of circumstances and seemingly insurmountable odds.

By the end of it, the union had pulled into its fight the entire U.S pharmaceutical industry, some of this country's highest-ranking politicians (including the president), and the Commonwealth of Puerto Rico. As one company official described it, the union transformed a garden variety plant closing into a federal case. It did so by turning its fight to save Whitehall jobs into a fight to stop the U.S. federal government from sponsoring job loss generally. What follows here is a case study of those events.

Case studies as analytical tools are limited in terms of the types of questions they can ask and answer. Clark (1989) has pointed out that "case studies are either too specific or too vague to make general observations about theory and other circumstances." However, empirical studies of labor disputes require a foundation of case studies by which general variables and study parameters can be determined. For example, an analyst could not determine the general impact of certain court actions or public relations maneuvers by unions in plant closing battles unless data existed about which battles employed those techniques. To that end, case studies are indispensable because the information contained in them contributes to the foundation of data necessary for future empirical analyses.

Moreover, and as Clark concedes, case studies can be "extraordinarily powerful" for examining difficult theoretical questions. There are perhaps many "difficult theoretical questions" which could be derived from the Whitehall plant closing campaign and "runaway plant" reform effort. The fundamental one examined here, however, is: how can relatively powerless groups in the United States influence broad governmental policy?

The analysis contained herein is based on research which included interviews with OCAW and AHP officials, thousands of pages of legal documents, Congressional and federal agency reports, mainland and Puerto Rico news accounts and union and company documents. The discussion of Puerto Rico's political and economic history focuses on the development of federal and insular tax incentives and is based on a variety of texts with differing perspectives on Puerto Rico's historical evolution. The discussion of OCAW's fight in the context of other union initiatives is based on the author's analysis of related labor texts and articles and conversations with labor leaders and scholars who specialize in areas relevant to this study.

I thank the Avetumian Fund for its generous financial support. Also, I am sincerely grateful for the invaluable comments and insights of Keith Knauss, Richard Leonard, Greg LeRoy, Connie Malloy, Ray Marshall, Thomas Nee, William Ruane, and Elliott Schwartz and for the thorough research assistance of Jason Gearheart. The views expressed here, however, are those of the author and should not necessarily be ascribed to the reviewers. In particular, AHP officials reject the connection made herein between OCAW's campaign and the 1993 Section 936 reforms.

I thank my editor, Robert McKenzie, who has been my champion throughout the many months of this endeavor. Thanks—you've been like a brother to me. Finally, thanks to my husband and sons who were so supportive and most importantly, patient, with this project and the commitment it required.

Exposing Federal Sponsorship of Job Loss

I

The Antagonists, the Issue and the Political and Economic Antecedents

This study examines an American plant closing, the union that fought it and the federal tax law that enabled it. The study chronicles an attempt by the Oil, Chemical and Atomic Workers (OCAW) union to avert the closure of Whitehall Laboratories in Elkhart, Indiana and to reform the federal tax law the union said caused the closure. OCAW's campaign began in the spring of 1990 and ended over three years later in August 1993.

Plant closings are a fact of life in market economies like the United States and likewise, attempts by unions, employees and local communities to avert them are recurrent and well-documented.[1] Naturally, and by necessity, fights to prevent plant closings are mostly local in scope even when the company is headquartered elsewhere and the reasons for the closing have little to do with the local situation. The effects of any single plant closing campaign rarely extend beyond the community immediately involved. The campaign analyzed here, however, had extraordinary national ramifications. Most notably, it touched off a Congressional tax reform effort which significantly scaled back a federal tax break worth billions to U.S. manufacturers. It also resulted in one of the few successful legislative attempts by organized labor to slow the exodus of so-called "runaway plants." This study examines how the union transformed a routine plant closing into a national debate over the U.S. government's role in displacing American jobs and then compelled Congressional action on the matter.

THE COMPANY AND THE UNION

In April 1990, New-York based American Home Products Corporation (AHP), one of the world's largest and most profitable pharmaceutical manufacturers, signaled it might close its Whitehall Laboratories production facility in Elkhart, Indiana. Whitehall, an AHP subsidiary established in 1926, had manufactured drugs in Elkhart since 1949. In 1990, the plant manufactured or packaged various over-the-counter medications including Anacin, Dristan, Preparation H, Primatene, Denorex, and Advil.

AHP was the world's seventh largest pharmaceutical manufacturer, with sales of nearly $6.8 billion.[2] It was the world's fifth most profitable pharmaceutical and ranked second when measured by profits as a percentage of assets.[3] In 1989, AHP's sales and earnings were at record levels and its dividends were up for the thirty ninth consecutive year. Also, until 1989 when it acquired A.H. Robins Company, the company carried no long-term debt, a notable characteristic in view of the preponderance of highly leveraged corporate acquisitions in the 1980's.[4]

AHP's success was representative of the growing good fortune of the U.S. pharmaceutical industry as a whole. Dubbed "investors' darlings" by financial analysts, drug makers' return on equity in 1990 was 26%, double the *Fortune 500* median.[5] Thanks to successful new drug introductions, price hikes on existing products, and aggressively innovative marketing, profits and gains in market share were spectacular. In addition to dominating sales in the states, U.S. pharmaceuticals enjoyed a solid presence worldwide, accounting for 42% of the major drugs marketed abroad.[6]

Whitehall Laboratories shared in the industry's success. The plant in Elkhart was one of several Whitehall manufacturing operations in the U.S. The various over-the-counter and personal care products manufactured there were profitable even as the sales of some declined. The physical plant was well-maintained and relatively efficient, although aging. The unionized work force was productive and cooperative, even compliant. Production and laboratory employees earned, on average, $13.48 per hour, [7] slightly higher than the industry average of $12.47,[8] and health and pension benefits were in line with industry standards.[9] Of the roughly 800 employees at Whitehall, approximately three-quarters were production workers and laboratory technicians represented by two local affiliates of the Oil, Chemical, and Atomic Workers (OCAW) union, Local 7-515 (production and maintenance) and Local 7-838 (laboratory).

Throughout its nearly 40 year history at the plant, OCAW never went on strike, contract negotiations were easy and union crossovers to company management positions were not uncommon. For its part, AHP never asked for a wage concession or any significant changes in work rules relating to productivity.[10] Labor/management relations at Whitehall were, for the most part, devoid of the divisiveness and rancor typical in some other unionized manufacturing environments. In fact, the relationship AHP managers had with union leadership up to 1990 could be characterized as friendly and paternalistic and seemed the very image of the "social accord" model of labor-management relations.[11]

PRELUDE TO A SHUTDOWN

1990 Contract Negotiations

Local union leaders first learned the company planned to close Whitehall during routine contract negotiations in April 1990. In a January coordinated bargaining session with the AFL-CIO's Industrial Union Department (IUD), a wage increase[12] was offered by AHP and accepted by the IUD and OCAW.[13] Subsequently, in April, the only issues left to discuss were those specific to the local unions in Elkhart.

When AHP[14] came to the table, the company's agenda was simple; AHP sought to remove a contract clause prohibiting it from moving production out of Elkhart.[15] This clause first showed up in the contract in 1960 and was the result of a deal struck to prevent the company from moving to Iowa.[16] In return, OCAW settled for a wage freeze. Although AHP eventually lifted the wage freeze, the relocation prohibition remained in the contract. Over the years, the clause was revised in minor ways but, for the most part and certainly in the most recent contract negotiations, the clause was not at issue. [17] In the April 1990 talks, it seemed to be the only issue.

Prior to 1990, local OCAW leaders enjoyed a friendly relationship with Whitehall and AHP managers. This friendliness was typical of labor-management relations throughout American Home's manufacturing facilities.[18] Furthermore, during the decade of the

1980's, mainstream U.S. labor leaders publicly pointed to American Home as a model of excellence in labor relations.[19] The OCAW-International Union (OCAW-IU) itself encouraged this view, even as recently as 1989, calling on AHP's senior vice president, Joseph Bock, to use his stature among managers and unionists alike to resolve a long and contentious strike between OCAW and a company unrelated to AHP. Lulled by the chumminess and loyalty they had come to expect from OCAW leaders, AHP negotiators assumed they could count on the union's continued acquiescence, even in the face of a shutdown.

AHP entered the April contract negotiating session believing it would be simply the first step in an orderly and smooth termination of production at the Elkhart facility. The company took steps to assure this eventuality by tipping off an OCAW-IU officer prior to the negotiating session that the shutdown was imminent. AHP viewed this tip-off as a favor to the union that would enable union leaders to concentrate on negotiating a better severance package for the workers who would be affected by the closure. Thus, AHP expected no resistance in the April 1990 negotiations.

Connie Malloy was the president of Local 7-515. She was new to the presidency, elected only four months earlier, when news of the shutdown came to light. In her 28 years at the plant, she had held various local leadership positions, including the vice-presidency. Considered a troublemaker by her foes, Malloy was nevertheless elected on a platform of change. She was only the second woman elected to the presidency of the union even though most of the unionized work force at Whitehall were women. Her gender and the recency of her position as local union president made her an outsider to the well-established relationships among local and international union leaders and company industrial relations executives. Comfortable in her outsider status, she had no use for the institutional history of her union's relationship with AHP and refused to take out the no-relocation clause. Perhaps because she was so new to the presidency, AHP officials may have presumed she had no real influence with union members and thus would be unlikely to garner support among them for her resistance to AHP's proposal. Or perhaps they thought she already had been informed of the possiblility of a shutdown by the OCAW-IU officer they had tipped off in March. Whatever the reason, AHP underestimated Malloy's reaction to its proposal to remove the no-relocation clause. The early April contract negotiations broke down over this clause and Malloy unilaterally decided to expose the company's plans to the press.

The Fight Begins

Malloy's revelation to the local press forced AHP to respond publicly. AHP assured employees that no decision had yet been made but it was "considering a phase out of its operations in Elkhart."[20] AHP mentioned it was conducting a study of all its operations to determine its production requirements. Behind the scenes, AHP made clear to union negotiators that if the anti-relocation language was not removed, it could choose to operate the plant without a contract, give them the requisite[21] 60 days notice and shut down the plant. When negotiations resumed in late April, OCAW acceded but requested inclusion of a provision requiring AHP to give 13 months' notice before the plant was closed. The union wanted pre notification a month before an official 12-month notification to the work force in which to "change [AHP's] mind or look at other avenues".[22] AHP consented and the contract was made.

To Malloy, the contract simply codified reality. The first negotiating session in early April "pre-notified" her to Whitehall's imminent closure. AHP's intentions could not have been clearer; the contract only formalized notification procedures. Malloy began the campaign to keep Whitehall open even before the parties returned to the bargaining table in late April.

What began as a rather haphazard, "we'll try anything" approach, soon evolved into a deliberate and effective legal, legislative and media strategy which ultimately resulted in an extraordinary $24 million settlement. Chapters Two and Three discuss and analyze these strategies and Chapter Four examines the details of the settlement. Moreover, although its attempt to keep the plant open eventually failed, the union did manage to expose a decades-old federal tax break it said was responsible for the transfer of Whitehall's and thousands more jobs from the states to Puerto Rico. This issue became the linchpin of the union's campaign.

Known as Section 936,[23] this Internal Revenue Code incentive, in effect, allowed U.S. parent companies to exempt from federal taxation some profits earned on their manufacturing operations in Puerto Rico. Over the years this tax break amounted to billions of dollars in tax savings for the pharmaceutical industry.[24] OCAW argued Section 936 subsidized the creation of jobs in Puerto Rico at the expense of jobs in the states and it used its struggle with AHP to exemplify this argument. The union launched a legislative reform effort in 1990, and in spite of intense lobbying by powerful supporters of Section 936, succeeded in effecting a significant reduction in Section 936 benefits three years later. OCAW's campaign to keep Whitehall open also touched off a national debate on the larger issue of the federal government's role generally in the "exporting" of American jobs.

How did OCAW convince federal legislators that its local problem was cause for alarm, especially when organized labor had so little Congressional support on any matter at the time? This is the fundamental question examined in Chapters Two and Three. After all, by 1990, a decade and a half of "corporate restructuring" had transformed the economy in the United States. Thousands of manufacturing facilities already had closed, taking with them millions of well-paying manufacturing jobs.[25] As high union wages persisted while real income for most other Americans fell, unions fell out of favor with Congress and the public who blamed them for the decline in competitiveness of U.S. firms.[26] The unfettered movement of capital was widely accepted as a natural and necessary element of a healthy market economy. In this context then, one local union's plant closing campaign seemed hardly remarkable and certainly held little promise for success. Indeed to many, including a sizable number of Whitehall employees and OCAW leaders, this was just one more desperate attempt to forestall the inevitable. Nevertheless, the Whitehall campaign was not to be a traditional union struggle, either in terms of its strategy or its outcome.

OCAW's decision to expand the scope of its efforts beyond the Whitehall closing differentiated it from other plant closing campaigns. Aware that a union's fight against a company was likely to be treated with disdain, if not ignored, by legislators, the press, and the public, OCAW broadened the definition of its struggle. Indeed, OCAW's leaders demonstrated remarkable savvy in fostering favorable press coverage of their campaign and enlisting support from a variety of interests. They raised the stakes of the plant closing by first challenging Section 936 in Congress and then by suing AHP and the Puerto Rican government under federal racketeering charges.

OCAW's leaders, at both the local and international levels, were uniquely suited to these tasks. Subsequent chapters discuss

OCAW's leadership of the campaign and examine why these unionists were able to take their fight with AHP to Capitol Hill and Puerto Rico. However, this discussion first requires an explanation of the connection between Section 936 and the pharmaceutical industry in Puerto Rico.

SECTION 936 AND THE PHARMACEUTICAL INDUSTRY IN PUERTO RICO

Section 936 of the Internal Revenue Code is a federal tax credit for U.S. corporations with operations in U.S. territorial possessions, including Puerto Rico. Almost invariably, these operations are wholly owned subsidiaries of U.S. "parent" corporations.[27] In 1990, Section 936 provided a tax credit equal to the federal tax liability on certain income earned by these operations, effectively exempting this income from federal taxation. Although the credit applied only to certain income and thus some profits were not exempt from federal taxation, the credit did exempt substantial income and as such yielded federal tax savings unavailable in and unparalleled by any other domestic tax jurisdiction.[28]

Section 936 evolved from a 1921 tax provision[29] which was enacted to promote investment in and enable U.S. firms to compete with their foreign counterparts in the Philippines.[30] This tax provision applied to other U.S. possessions as well, including Puerto Rico. In Puerto Rico, the island government also enacted complementary local tax incentives[31] and together with the federal tax credit, they helped transform the Puerto Rico economy from one dominated by agriculture to one based on manufacturing, government, services and construction. Initially, labor-intensive industries dominated the manufacturing sector. Gradually, though, the pattern of expansion shifted toward higher technology, capital-intensive manufacturing, including the production of pharmaceuticals.[32]

Economists attribute this concentration of capital-intensive manufacturing to incentives accorded by Section 936 tax provisions (and its predecessors) and to other economic conditions in Puerto Rico.[33] First, Section 936 allowed U.S. mainland corporations to transfer intangible assets, such as patents and trademarks, to subsidiaries in Puerto Rico. Firms could deduct the cost of producing intangible assets from their mainland tax liability, where tax rates are higher and the deduction is more valuable. The income from those transferred assets could appear on the subsidiary's books and thus be taxed at the much lower tax rate in Puerto Rico.[34] Pharmaceutical manufacturers were particularly well-suited to taking advantage of this tax shelter, due to their high marketing costs (which create marketing intangibles) and high research and development costs (which generate manufacturing intangibles).[35]

Another reason capital-intensive rather than labor-intensive manufacturers located in Puerto Rico was the island's higher wage rate relative to other Caribbean countries. Although average manufacturing labor costs were lower in Puerto Rico than in any state in the U.S., manufacturing wages were higher than most alternative low-tax locations.[36] The minimum wage established by the U.S. Congress for mainland employers also applied to Puerto Rico. Therefore, other countries with lower wage rates had a comparative advantage relative to Puerto Rico in attracting labor-intensive industry.[37] In 1989, the average hourly wage for a pharmaceutical worker in Puerto Rico was $8.76,[38] on the mainland, it was $12.47.[39]

In 1989, every major U.S. drug and pharmaceutical manufacturer had production facilities in Puerto Rico. In all, 77 facilities were involved in the manufacture of pharmaceutical products and all but 15 were owned by U.S. companies. Sixteen of the U.S. companies operating in Puerto Rico were listed in the *Fortune 500*. In total, this industry directly employed nearly 17,000 workers[40] accounting for roughly 18% of the total Section 936-related employment in Puerto Rico.[41]

American Home Products Corporation was the last among major pharmaceutical manufacturers to locate a production facility in Puerto Rico, opening its first facility there in 1984.[42] By 1989, it employed approximately 1,000 people at two production facilities.[43]

THE POLITICAL ENVIRONMENT, 1990-1993

The battle over the closure of Whitehall Laboratories had significance far beyond the environs of Elkhart, Indiana. OCAW didn't simply challenge AHP's plant closing decision; they took on the system that enabled it. Many powerful interests had a lot to lose by what the union proposed. It stands to reason that for any progress to be made toward those ends, OCAW had to engage the support of equally powerful interests. The following section points out these interests not to play down OCAW's role or to suggest it was simply lucky, but rather to take this analysis beyond a David and Goliath-type characterization. Merely to describe the union's strategies and ascribe their accomplishments to either heroism or organizational and tactical acuity would be to reveal a fundamental misunderstanding of the power of unions in the United States. Relative to a company the size and prosperity of American Home, OCAW was nearly powerless. To accomplish anything, it needed to invoke the power of other interests and bring their influence to bear on its cause. This OCAW did, as Chapters Two and Three show. Nonetheless, to describe its campaign without defining the political context would reduce this analysis to a simple lesson in public relations.

There was a unique combination of political and economic circumstances at the time of the plant closing announcement which provided the union opportunities to transform its local situation into a national issue. A serendipitous convergence of events, that couldn't have been foreseen either by AHP or OCAW, set the stage for this transformation. The following sections outline these attendant political circumstances that ultimately were brought to bear on the union's plant closing campaign and Section 936 reform effort.

The significance of these circumstances to the outcome of the union's efforts cannot be overstated. To the extent that their struggle could be called successful, OCAW was lucky to have been handed this moment in time. After all, the issues the union raised were not particularly novel. U.S. organized labor had protested without success for years over the loss of well-paying manufacturing jobs to Mexico but was unable to seriously challenge the tariff laws[44] which encouraged this job movement. Moreover, organized labor, including OCAW, had targeted Section 936 for reform long before the Whitehall closing, but to no avail. In 1990, however, suddenly the time was right; politicians, the media and the public were willing to listen to the concerns of a union.

1990 Congressional Election

In 1990, John Hiler, the Congressman for Elkhart, was in the midst of a campaign for reelection to a sixth term in the U.S. House of Representatives. When AHP announced its shutdown intentions in

April of that year, Malloy immediately characterized the closing as a federally-sponsored transfer of jobs to Puerto Rico and appealed to Hiler for help.[45] His initial response was lukewarm and she publicly accused Hiler of caring more about Puerto Ricans than about his own constituents.[46] Compelled to respond to Malloy's accusation, Hiler, within days of AHP's announcement of a possible shutdown, drafted and introduced legislation to reform Section 936.

While some observers[47] characterized this action as nothing more than political expediency, Hiler, a Republican, defended it as entirely consistent with his advocacy of *laissez-faire* economic policies. He argued he could support the reform of Section 936 on the grounds that it was improper for the federal government to interfere legislatively with the marketplace.[48] This view paralleled OCAW's argument that the federal government should not underwrite with tax revenues the relocation of jobs from one U.S. location to another.

Even though Hiler was serving his fifth term in Congress, his reelection in 1990 was not assured. In fact, he lost the 1990 election to Democrat, Timothy Roemer. In 1988, Hiler had won by a very narrow margin after a campaign in which his opponent blamed him for not doing enough to prevent the closing of several other large local manufacturers. In light of his vulnerability on this issue, the Whitehall shutdown was politically fortuitous because it offered Hiler an opportunity to side with organized labor. He could fight a plant closing while remaining true to his personal politics and in a way that would not alienate his Republican supporters. Thus, ironically, a conservative Republican was the first legislator to carry labor's view to Congress and target Section 936 on the basis of job relocation. Chapter Two discusses whether his position as a Republican helped or hindered OCAW's Section 936 reform bid. Hiler's efficacy notwithstanding, the union clearly benefited by the occasion of the 1990 Congressional election and by Hiler's paradoxical willingness to act on labor's behalf.

Congressional Priorities

In 1990, the budget deficit of the United States was $278 billion, a record peacetime high in both absolute and relative (as a percentage of GDP) terms.[49] By 1992, it had grown to $340 billion.[50] Congress had expressed concern over the budget deficit as far back as the middle 1970's. It enacted various pieces of legislation over the years to address the problem but with negligible success.[51] In the period 1990 through 1993, the political pressure to cut the deficit grew in lockstep with the deficit itself. Tax expenditures[52], as well as direct spending, came under scrutiny as potential sources for increased revenues to reduce the deficit.[53]

The Department of the Treasury, in its periodic reports on the operation and effect of the possessions system of taxation, identified Section 936 as a tax expenditure and counted the tax credits taken by possessions corporations[54] as direct losses to the Treasury. Puerto Rico government officials and others interested in retaining Section 936 vigorously opposed this characterization. They argued it was inaccurate to count the uncollected corporate income taxes as the "cost" of the incentive to the Treasury because such accounting assumes that, in the absence of Section 936, the taxes would be collected. Section 936 proponents maintained that because Treasury does not characterize foreign income tax credits as tax expenditures, Treasury should not count Section 936 credits as such either.[55] Furthermore, they said, the Treasury reports did not fully account for the offsetting benefits of the tax incentive to the island's economy[56] or to the U.S. economy. [57]

Regardless of the objections by proponents of Section 936, however, the Treasury reports defined the issues in Congress before 1990. Congress scaled back Section 936 benefits in 1976, 1982 and 1986 based largely on budgetary problems and tax sheltering abuses outlined in the Treasury reports. As a result of the sixth Treasury report, Congress believed Section 936 not only cost the Treasury over $2.6 billion annually but that it was particularly inefficient because it cost taxpayers, on average, $58,000 to create a pharmaceutical job that paid $16,000.[58] As a budgetary matter, therefore, Section 936 was open for discussion in 1990.

Professional and Middle-Management Unemployment in the United States

The U.S. economic recession in 1990-1991[59] differed from previous downturns in that for the first time on record more white-collar workers were laid-off than blue-collar workers.[60] Also, an American Management Association survey in 1991 showed that while middle managers made up only five to eight percent of the work force, they accounted for more than 17 percent of all dismissals in the prior three years.[61] The financial press was replete with stories of formerly well-paid and highly qualified professionals who suddenly found themselves laid off in the latest round of corporate downsizing.

The problems of this new class of unemployed worker could not be blamed on a lack of skills or education. Education and training were supposed to have insulated workers from economic downturns or at least assured them of remaining employable. However, re-employment prospects for these workers were more remote than in previous recessions. Permanent separations accounted for 85 percent of job losses in the 1990-91 recession compared with 56 percent in four previous downturns.[62] As Columbia University professor Katherine Newman explained, "if credentials, skills and education can't protect you, then there is no recipe for security in the American job market."[63] Well-educated and highly skilled jobless Americans wanted to know why they were failing when they had played by all the rules.

One measure of the breadth of this interest can be found in the success of the book, *America: What Went Wrong,* by Donald Barlett and James Steele.[64] This book was a reprint of a series that appeared in the *Philadelphia Inquirer* in 1991 which examined the American tax system and showed how changes to the federal tax code in the 1980's resulted in a restructuring of the U.S economy at the expense of middle-class, taxpaying Americans. Before the series was published in book form, the *Inquirer* filled over 400,000 requests for reprints of the articles.[65] This was the greatest reader response to a series the paper had ever received.[66] After the book was published, it was on the *New York Times* bestseller list for 31 straight weeks in 1992.[67]

This search by Americans and their representatives in Congress for answers to unprecedented economic troubles created a window of opportunity for the union to make its case to a broader audience. OCAW connected mainland job losses with a federal tax system gone awry and held up Section 936 as one of the system's most egregious examples.

1992 Presidential Election Campaign

Presidential campaigns in the United States tend to force Americans to examine collectively broad national policy issues more intensively and seriously than at any other time. Candidates discuss the "direction" in which the country is headed offering explanations for the current state of affairs and solutions to the country's problems. The press covers these discussions and the immediacy of the impending election deadline compels voters to engage, at some level, in the discussions and decide whom they think is right. In effect, the campaign draws voters into a national debate over governmental policies.

Some political analysts argue that in the 1992 presidential campaign, voters shaped the debates more than ever before.[68] Whether this is true or not, voters did enjoy unprecedented access to the debate, made possible by the willingness of most of the candidates to converse directly with voters on live, nationally broadcast television and radio "talk shows." Some analysts contend that while the press seemed preoccupied with covering the personal weaknesses of the candidates, voters in these live settings tended to insist on discussing the "issues." National opinion polls throughout the campaign cited jobs and the federal budget deficit as the "issues" about which voters were the most concerned. Where did all the middle class jobs go and where would they come from in the future? Was the federal government to blame and if so, what were the specific policies that brought us to this point? Even if the federal government could stimulate job growth, how could we afford it in light of the budget deficit?

In other words, the 1992 presidential campaign provided a forum for the electorate to discuss broad economic policy questions and examine the implications of federal policies on jobs and the deficit. The campaign was important to OCAW's efforts because the union could use the opportunity to take its case to the press and characterize its situation as representative of what was "wrong with America." In this context, even a tax law as arcane and complicated as Section 936 was open to question.

Prior to the early 1990's, a relatively small group of economists, academics, legislators and special interests took an interest in constraining the tax advantages of Section 936. Opponents of Section 936 counted the costs of the law primarily in budgetary terms. The wider mainland public was, for the most part, unaware of and unconcerned with this tax incentive. OCAW, however, brought to light the law's human consequences. OCAW's characterization simplified the definition of Section 936 and its role in mainland job displacement. Though candidates did not point exclusively to Section 936 *per se* (they tended to refer more generally to federal policies that promoted the "exporting" of U.S. jobs), the federal government's role in causing mainland job loss was a campaign issue.[69] This high-level dialogue significantly improved OCAW's chances for Congressional action on its Section 936 reform legislation.

The union made the most of the heightened interest in employment and deficit reduction policies created by the occasion of the presidential campaign. Chapter Three examines OCAW's remarkable media and public relations operation and Chapters Two and Three discuss its lobbying effort on behalf of Section 936 reform. These chapters demonstrate further how OCAW's battle to keep Whitehall open connected mainland job displacement with Section 936 and ultimately made it a matter of concern for the president of the United States.

Health Care Reform and the Attack on the Pharmaceutical Industry

After jobs and the deficit, health care reform was the issue American voters cared about most during the 1992 presidential campaign.[70] The United States was in the middle of a recession in this period and over 34 million Americans had no health insurance. At the same time, the pharmaceutical industry thrived and reported record sales and profits. The coincidence of these conditions made the pharmaceutical industry a target for blame; consequently, the industry was attacked in the press and on Capitol Hill. Leading the attack in the U.S. Congress was Senator David Pryor, a Democrat from Arkansas, Chairman for the Senate Special Committee on Aging.

Pryor criticized the pharmaceutical industry's profits as exploitative and oligopolistic. U.S. pharmaceutical firms benefited more than any other industry in Puerto Rico from Section 936 tax treatment; for this reason, Pryor made Section 936 reform one of his priorities. Although he is a Democrat, Pryor was not an unequivocal friend of organized labor. Pryor's interest in Section 936 reform was based on his view that this tax incentive was nothing but "corporate welfare" for an industry that needed it the least of all. He characterized it as "the mother of all tax breaks" and led the fight in Congress to repeal Section 936.

The prominence of health care reform as a national issue and the concomitant attack on the pharmaceutical industry by Congress and the press, paved the way for the union's media campaign and its

Section 936 reform bid in Congress. It was relatively easy for OCAW to depict AHP as the villain and to characterize the plant closing as unnecessary and greedy because pharmaceutical companies were so profitable while the rest of the economy suffered. OCAW's characterization was consistent with the drug industry-as-pariah image already being extolled by the press and some legislators. The shutdown conveniently provided pharmaceutical industry antagonists with a set of victims to dramatize and personify their point of view. The plight of laid-off Whitehall workers was neither unique nor particularly newsworthy; but because it seemed to represent this larger, more pressing national problem, it grew in significance.

Puerto Rico Statehood Plebiscite

In 1990, at the time of the Whitehall plant closing announcement, Puerto Ricans were embroiled in a debate over their political status with regard to the United States. At issue was whether Puerto Rico should retain its commonwealth status, become the 51st state, or be an independent nation. Advocates on all sides of the argument urged members of the U.S. Congress to authorize a plebiscite regarding Puerto Rico's status, the results of which would be binding.[71] Ultimately, a vote was mandated but the law did not bind Congress to accept the results.

Section 936 was central to the question of Puerto Rico's status. Section 936 was a powerful incentive in attracting firms that otherwise would not be interested in locating on the island. As such, it was the bedrock of Puerto Rico's modern economic development and its economy. If Puerto Rico were to become either a state or an independent nation, it would lose Section 936 tax benefits. In the case of statehood, the U.S. Internal Revenue Code would apply to Puerto Rico in the same way it applies to the other states[72] and resident Puerto Rican individuals and firms would become subject to U.S. federal taxation.[73]

If Puerto Rico were an independent nation, Section 936 would not apply and U.S. firms would lose this tax credit against their U.S. tax liability. Their earnings would be taxed in the same way other foreign earnings are. The U.S. foreign tax credit would apply and the relative value of this credit versus the 936 credit would depend upon the corporate tax rate Puerto Rico imposed.

For both statehood and independence advocates, Section 936 was an obstacle to the political changes they sought. If Section 936 were eliminated by Congressional action, the most significant economic argument *against* independence or statehood would have been eliminated. Thus, the union's effort to amend Section 936 was well received by both statehood and independence advocates in Puerto Rico. The union targeted the highest ranking Puerto Rico government officials, going so far as to sue the governor for illegal acts relating to his administration of Section 936. This unprecedented legal action and OCAW's legislative attack on Section 936 generated intense press coverage by the Puerto Rico and Caribbean media; they were ready-made story "angles" for discussing Puerto Rico's future.

OCAW's actions held up for public scrutiny issues important to statehood and independence advocates. In effect, OCAW gave voice and added clout to their positions on Puerto Rico's status. This was especially true with regard to OCAW's Section 936 reform attempt. Statehooders and *independentistas* pointed to it as proof that Puerto Rico was bound to lose the tax break in any case, that commonwealth status was no guarantee against this eventuality.

OCAW garnered assistance in Puerto Rico that would not have been available had Puerto Ricans not been in the throes of deciding their political and economic future with the United States. Chapters Two and Three discuss why this assistance was critical to the outcome of OCAW's lawsuits and tax reform effort.

NOTES

1   See for example, Harold E. Way and Carla Weiss, comps., *Plant Closings: A Selected Bibliography of Materials Published through 1985* (Ithaca, New York: Martin P. Catherwood Library, NYSSILR, Cornell Univ., Sept. 1987); Carla Weiss, comp., *Plant Closings: A Selected Bibliography of Materials Published 1986 through 1990* (Ithaca, New York: Martin P. Catherwood Library, NYSSILR, Cornell Univ., 1991); Charles Craypo and Bruce Nissen, eds., *Grand Designs: The Impact of Corporate Strategies on Workers, Unions, and Communities* (Ithaca, N.Y.: ILR Press, 1993); John Portz, *The Politics of Plant Closings* (Lawrence, Kan.: University Press of Kansas, 1990); Carolyn C. Perruci et al., *Plant Closings:*

International Context and Social Costs (New York: Aldine de Gruyter, 1988); Eric Mann, *Taking on General Motors: A Case Study of the UAW Campaign to Keep GM Van Nuys Open* (Los Angeles: Institute of Industrial Relations Publications, Univ. of California, 1987).

2   American Home Products Corporation, *Annual Report 1989* (Madison, N.J.: American Home Products Corporation), p. 32.

3   Brian O'Reilly, "Drugmakers Under Attack," *Fortune*, 29 July 1991, p. 273.

4   By the end of 1991, the $2 billion of commercial paper issued by the company in connection with the merger all had been reclassified to current liabilities. (American Home Products Corporation, *Annual Reports 1988, 1989, 1990, 1991* (Madison, NJ.: American Home Products Corporation))

5   O'Reilly, "Drugmakers," p. 48.

6   Ibid., p. 50.

7   Oil, Chemical and Atomic Workers Union, "OCAW Comparison and Analysis of Drug and Cosmetic Groups Selected Contract Provisions," (Prepared by OCAW for the Drug and Cosmetic Council Meeting, Washington D.C., June 18-22, 1989), p. 1.

8   U.S. Department of Labor, Bureau of Labor Statistics, *Employment and Earnings* (Washington, D.C.: GPO, August 1992), p.124.

9   Oil, Chemical and Atomic Workers Union, "OCAW Comparison," pp. 6, 9, 12, 15.

10   Connie Malloy, "Taking on American Home Products: A Description and Analysis of the Fight to Keep Whitehall Open" (manuscript, Indiana University at South Bend, 1991), p. 1.1. Also, Charles Weisweaver, interview by author, Mishawaka, Ind., 24 January 1994. Mr. Weisweaver is a former OCAW Local 7-515 president.

11   The "social accord" model of labor-management relations has been defined in a variety of ways. Bruce Nissen analyzes some of the definitions in Nissen, "A Post-World War II "Social Accord?" in *U.S. Labor Relations, 1945-1989: Accommodation and Conflict,* ed. Bruce Nissen (New York: Garland Publishing, 1990).

12   Three percent annually over the four years of the contract. This increase was nearly identical to the wage increase offered and accepted in the 1986 contract.

13 Over the strong objections of Connie Malloy who was dissatisfied
    with the company's health benefits concession demands. Malloy
    ultimately voted to accept the company's wage and benefits package
    but only after it was clear her dissenting vote would not change the
    outcome of the vote in this coordinated bargaining session.
14 For the sake of simplicity, throughout this study company decisions
    and actions will be attributed to "AHP."
15 The clause read "the Company agrees to continue to operate within
    the general area of Elkhart until the expiration of this agreement," in
    "Agreement between Whitehall Laboratories, Inc. and Local No. 7-
    515 Oil, Chemical and Atomic Workers International Union AFL-
    CIO," effective September 15, 1986, Article I.2.A, p. 2.
16 Weisweaver, interview.
17 A survey of the prevalence of plant shutdown or relocation
    restrictions in union contracts in the United States shows that in
    1989, roughly 25% of union contracts contained such restrictions.
    (Bureau of National Affairs, Inc., *Basic Patterns in Union
    Contracts* (Washington, D.C.: BNA Books, 1989), p. 81.) Also, this
    no-relocation clause was not normally a part of other AHP union
    contracts, according to company representatives.
18 At the time of the Whitehall closing announcement, AHP had
    roughly 30 labor contracts worldwide with various AFL-CIO
    affiliates and independent locals.
19 See Chapter IV for further explanation and references.
20 Jim Miller, "Whitehall union now negotiating," *Elkhart (Indiana)
    Truth,* 27 April 1990.
21 A federal statute, the Worker Adjustment and Retraining
    Notification Act (WARN Act), required AHP to notify Whitehall
    employees 60 days in advance of a permanent plant shutdown. See
    Chapter II for further information about this law and how it
    pertained to the Whitehall shutdown.
22 "Negotiations 1990: Joint Session #2 with Locals 7-515 and 7-838,"
    (American Home Products Meeting transcript, April 30, 1990), p. 3.
23 Public Law 99-514, 100 Stat. 2085
24 U.S. General Accounting Office, *Tax Policy: Puerto Rico and the
    Section 936 Tax Credit* (Washington, D.C.: GAO/GGD-93-109,
    June 1993), p. 48.
25 Portz, *Politics,* p. vii.

26 David Brody, *Workers in Industrial America: Essays on the Twentieth Century Struggle* (New York: Oxford University Press, 1980), p.239. For other analyses of the state of unionism in the U.S., see Michael Goldfield, *The Decline of Organized Labor in the United States* (Chicago: University of Chicago Press, 1987); Ray F. Marshall, *Unheard Voices: Labor and Economic Policy in a Competitive World* (New York: Basic Books, 1987); Lawrence R. Mishel and Paula Voos eds., *Unions and Economic Competitiveness* (Armonk, N.Y.: M.E. Sharpe, 1992); Gordon L. Clark, *Unions and Communities Under Siege: American Communities and the Crisis of Organized Labor* (New York: Cambridge University Press, 1989).

27 Congressional Budget Office, *Potential Economic Impacts of Changes in Puerto Rico's Status Under S. 712* (Washington, D.C.: GPO, April 1990), p. 5.

28 See 50/50 profit-split explanation in U.S. Department of the Treasury, *Operation and Effect of the Possessions Corporation System of Taxation, Sixth Report* (Washington, D.C.:GPO, March 1989), p. 10.

29 C. 136, 42 Stat. 227

30 Nancy H. Kaufman, "Do the TEFRA Amendments Go Too Far?" *Wisconsin Law Review*, 2 (1984):533.

31 See Chapter II for further explanation of Puerto Rico's tax incentives.

32 Congressional Budget Office, *Potential Economic Impacts,* p. 6. Also see Price Waterhouse, "Benefits and Costs of Section 936," (Washington, D.C.: Prepared for Puerto Rico, U.S.A. Foundation, May 1991), vol. I, pp. 38-52.

33 U.S. Department of the Treasury, *Operation and Effect of the Possessions Corporation System of Taxation, Sixth Report* (Washington D.C.: GPO, March 1989), p. 36.

34 The Tax Equity and Fiscal Responsibility Act of 1982 (TEFRA) provided statutory rules for the allocation to a possessions corporation of income from intangibles to "lessen the abuse caused by taxpayers claiming tax-free income generated by intangibles developed outside of Puerto Rico." (Treasury, *Sixth Report*, p. 8, quoting Joint Committee on Taxation, *General Explanation of the Revenue Provisions of the Tax Equity and Fiscal Responsibility Act of 1982,* December 1982, pp. 81-83.)

35 Congressional Budget Office, *Potential Economic Impacts,* p. 7.

36 Price Waterhouse, *Benefits and Costs,* vol. I, table III.A.-4, p. 45.

37 In 1974, the U.S. Congress imposed automatic periodic increases in the Puerto Rico minimum wage to bring the minimum wage in Puerto Rico up to the U.S. level. By 1981, the minimum wage in Puerto Rico had reached U.S. levels in nearly all industries. The parity in U.S. and Puerto Rico minimum wages ended in 1991 however when an increase in the U.S. level did not apply equally to Puerto Rico. Nevertheless, the relatively high wage rate in Puerto Rico as compared to other Caribbean manufacturing locations persists despite the disparity between U.S. and Puerto Rico levels. (Price Waterhouse, *Benefits and Costs,* vol. I, p. 38.)

38 Puerto Rico Department of Labor and Human Resources, *Census of Manufacturing Industries of Puerto Rico,* 1990.

39 U.S. Department of Labor, *Employment and Earnings,* p. 124.

40 Commonwealth of Puerto Rico, The Economic Development Administration, "Highlights of the Drug and Pharmaceutical Industry in Puerto Rico" (RCM9902.5/796), September 1990.

41 U.S. General Accounting Office, *Pharmaceutical Industry: Tax Benefits of Operating in Puerto Rico* (Washington, D.C.: GAO/GGD-92-72BR, May 1992), p. 4.

42 Smith Barney, Harris Upham & Co., Inc., "American Home Products Company Report," file 545, report no. 1004740, INVESTEXT, 26 April 1990, p. 2.

43 U.S General Accounting Office, *Pharmaceutical Industry,* p. 18. OCAW disputes the GAO's estimate and claims AHP's Puerto Rico employment in 1989 was closer to 1,300.

44 For example, provisions 9802.00.60 and 9802.00.80 of the Harmonized Tariff Schedule (formerly known as Items 806.30 and 807.00 of the Tariff Schedules of the United States).

45 Hiler first was confronted publicly with the possibility of a Whitehall shutdown on a local call-in television show. A union member called in to ask Hiler for his reaction. Malloy heard from this union member that Hiler essentially defended Section 936 because of high unemployment in Puerto Rico. This hearsay report angered Malloy and she accused Hiler to the press of having more concern for Puerto Ricans than for his own constituents in the Third District of Indiana. Hiler then contacted Malloy to offer his assistance. This was their first direct contact on the matter.

46 The *South Bend Tribune* quoted Malloy "quoting" Hiler, "He (Hiler) was absolutely no help. He said, 'Those people are poor down there (Puerto Rico), they need jobs.'" (Jeff Kurowski, "Future murkier at Whitehall plant," *South Bend (Indiana) Tribune,* 27 April 1990.) In editorials to the paper in the days following, angry readers cited Malloy's "quote" and accused Hiler of "turning [his] back on the people" and threatening to "remember this come election time."("Will anyone fight for jobs?" *Elkhart Truth,* 30 April 1990 and "Hiler no help to Whitehall union," *South Bend Tribune,* 30 April 1990.)

47 Letter to the Editor, "Elkhart Whitehall plant workers lucky this is an election year," *South Bend Tribune,* 8 June 1990.

48 Editorial, "Whitehall jobs worth fight," *Elkhart Truth,* 13 May 1990 and Jeff Kurowski, "Hiler weighs in on unions' [sic] side in plant moves," *South Bend Tribune,* 12 May 1990. Also, John Hiler, interview by author, 21 January 1994.

49 Congressional Budget Office, *Reducing the Deficit: Spending and Revenue Options* (A Report to the Senate and House Committees on the Budget, Washington, D.C.: GPO, February 1993), p. 4. Economists use different measures of the deficit. The deficit measure quoted here is the "on-budget deficit" as defined by the Congressional Budget Office. The on-budget deficit excludes the transactions of the Social Security trust funds and the Postal Service from the deficit calculations. Including these funds results in a lower deficit estimate.

50 Ibid.

51 Ibid., pp. 3-6.

52 "Tax expenditures" are defined as tax revenues foregone because of tax provisions that either are enacted to serve as incentives for the private sector of the economy or have that effect. The tax incentives (like Section 936) are designed to encourage certain kinds of economic behavior and are used in lieu of direct governmental expenditures to achieve a particular objective. The term "tax expenditure" was coined by Stanley Surrey when he was assistant secretary of the treasury for tax policy in the early 1970's. (Martin Feldstein, "A Contribution to the Theory of Tax Expenditures: The Case of Charitable Giving," in *The Economics of Taxation,* eds. Henry J. Aaron and Michael J. Boskin (Washington, D.C.: The Brookings Institution, 1980), p. 101.)

53 In the 1970's, policy makers began to question and debate the efficacy and efficiency of tax expenditures as policy instruments. This debate pointed out the lack of accounting for tax expenditures in the federal budget. Congress enacted a number of measures during this period to more clearly identify and quantify the impact of tax and direct expenditures on the federal budget. One provision, which was mandated as part of the Tax Reform Act of 1976, required the Treasury to submit an annual report that analyzes the operation and effect of the possessions corporation system of taxation. (Public Law 94-455) Subsequently, Congress specified that the report be issued every two years. Most recently, the reports are issued every four or so years and partly because of limitations on the availability of tax return data, the reports analyze data from five or six years prior to the year they are issued.

54 Possessions corporations, as defined by the Department of the Treasury, are "U.S.-chartered companies that are effectively exempt under Section 936 [prior to 1993] of the Internal Revenue Code from federal tax on business income and qualified passive investment income from Puerto Rico and certain other U.S. possessions." (Treasury, *Sixth Report*, p. 1)

55 Price Waterhouse, *Benefits and Costs*, vol. I, pp. 65-71.

56 Nelson Famadas, "Section 936: Myths and Realities," in *Puerto Rico: The Search for a National Policy*, ed. Richard J. Bloomfield (Boulder, Colo.: Westview Press, Inc., 1985), p. 74.

57 Price Waterhouse, *Benefits and Costs*, vol. I, pp. 9-35.

58 Treasury, *Sixth Report*, table 4-6, p. 47.

59 U.S. Department of Commerce, Bureau of the Census, *Statistical Abstracts of the United States, 1993* (Washington, D.C.: GPO), table 690, p. 442.

60 David Hage, Linda Grant, Jim Impoco, "White Collar Wasteland," *U.S. News & World Report*, 28 June 1993.

61 Anne B. Fisher, "Morale Crisis," *Fortune*, 18 November 1991, p. 71.

62 Hage, et al., "White Collar Wasteland," p. 44.

63 Ibid.

64 Donald Barlett and James Steele, *America: What Went Wrong?* (Kansas City, Mo.: Andrews & McMeel, 1991).

65 Donald Barlett, interview by author, 16 December 1994.

66 Barlett and Steele, *America: What Went Wrong?* p. vii.

67 *New York Times Book Review,* 22 November 1992.
68 Joe Klein, "The Year of the Voter," *Newsweek,* Special Election Edition, November/December 1992, p. 14.
69 Chapters Two and Three discuss this point in greater depth.
70 Klein, *Newsweek,* p. 10.
71 A bill introduced in the Senate, S712, was under consideration by Congress and if adopted would have made the results of the status referendum binding.
72 Although elimination of Section 936 benefits could be phased in rather than done immediately, as suggested by S712.
73 Congressional Budget Office, *Potential Economic Impacts.* This report outlines various consequences of a change in status for Puerto Rico.

II

Obsolescence of the Picket Line:
Taking the Battle to the Courts and
Capitol Hill

"There's nothing unusual about this plant closure. What is
unusual is the reaction to it." Louis L. Hoynes, Jr., AHP Senior
Vice President and General Counsel[1]

A plant closure is the ultimate crisis for workers and it
inherently is the situation in which a union has the fewest response
options. If a union chooses to fight a plant closing, its most powerful
weapon, the ability to withhold work, is irrelevant and useless. Without
this weapon, the union is left with several options: to respond with
collective actions, such as rallies, picket lines, boycotts, and union
meetings, to attempt a joint labor-management turnaround or an
employee buyout, or to mobilize governmental influence.

A collective action, such as a boycott, is unlikely to avert a
plant closure unless it is massive and widespread. Because a single
plant closing is viewed primarily as a local problem, a collective action
is unlikely to elicit sufficient support to reverse a firm's closure
decision. Even locally, a union's fight to "save jobs" encounters
resistance. Community leaders are eager to maintain a "hospitable"
environment for doing business and citizens are apathetic and generally
suspicious of unions. When the local collective actions fail to avert a
closure, the union shows itself to be weak and anachronistic.

Likewise, a union faces many obstacles in mobilizing
governmental influence. "Governmental influence" means not only the
power of elected officials and bureaucrats but also the power of laws
and regulations. It is not illegal to close a plant and there are very few

25

laws governing plant closures in the United States. Thus, legal challenges are rare.[2] Similarly, to change or enact legislation is a lengthy endeavor and one that is not likely, by itself, to avert a particular closure.

Unions face different but equally challenging obstacles in mobilizing action by government officials. Elected officials may be unwilling, for political reasons, or unable, because of financial or policy constraints, to join a union's efforts to avert a plant closure. As a result, a union can be left with no viable response, and again, it appears impotent and inconsequential.

OCAW's Whitehall plant closing battle was different. OCAW identified several possible judicial remedies early in its campaign and ultimately brought twelve federal legal actions. It blamed a federal tax law for the closure and enlisted local and federal elected officials to change the law. It rallied broad national interest to its cause not through traditional collective action but by a sophisticated media and public relations campaign. In short, it overcame many of the obstacles that typically derail a union's attempts to affect a plant closure.

Nevertheless, and in spite of the union's innovative efforts, the Whitehall plant in Elkhart closed on schedule. However, OCAW did win a substantial financial settlement as a result of its lawsuits. Moreover, the U.S. Congress ultimately cut back the lucrative benefits to corporations of the tax law the union blamed for the closure. OCAW's use of judicial and legislative redress, while not unprecedented, was uncommonly successful. Because it succeeded in ways other unions have not, OCAW's approach is analyzed here.

THE ISSUE

OCAW's fight to keep Whitehall open did not begin with a grand design, a "corporate campaign", or a sophisticated legal or lobbying plan; it began with Connie Malloy. Malloy simply came out of the April 1990 contract negotiations fighting with little consideration given to the costs and risks inherent in such a fight. She did not work out beforehand that the time was right for an attack on Section 936; she simply told the press what she believed was the truth, that AHP was moving Whitehall's production to Puerto Rico to take advantage of the tax credits afforded by Section 936. In 1988, she had watched while Elkhart   packaging   equipment   was   crated   and   shipped to a new Whitehall plant in Puerto Rico and then waited in vain for promised new production lines to arrive. She heard then about Section 936 and gut instinct told her the law threatened Whitehall's future and was fundamentally unfair to mainland workers.

Even so, AHP's shutdown speculation caught Malloy off guard. She had been lulled by AHP's financial robustness and thought Elkhart would be spared because of its history of labor-management peace. When it was clear these considerations had not figured significantly into AHP's decision to close Whitehall, only the Section 936 explanation made sense to her. Malloy articulated the connection between the law and the imminent Whitehall closure simply and unequivocally, and argued it was wrong for the federal government to use workers' own tax dollars to underwrite the elimination of their jobs. Her concise and compelling definition characterized the debate and was the foundation for OCAW's legal and legislative strategy.

Congressional Support

Even as AHP continued to insist that its closure decision was still under consideration, Malloy began to pressure U.S. Representative John Hiler to introduce legislation to repeal Section 936. Several Local 7-515 members wrote letters to members of Congress and Malloy publicly maligned Hiler, accusing him of caring more about Puerto Ricans than his own constituents.[3] Within days of Malloy's public warning that a shutdown was imminent, Hiler introduced the American Jobs Stability Act of 1990.[4] This federal legislation sought to prohibit Section 936 tax benefits to firms that were simply transferring jobs from the mainland to Puerto Rico. Hiler's legislation represented a startling elevation of the stakes of the Whitehall plant closing battle.

Indeed, Hiler's legislation gave this campaign substance and took it beyond the traditional picket lines and local union hall. First, it provided the union an immediate platform and was a powerful rallying device. Even though some Whitehall workers were skeptical of Hiler's political motives and held little hope for the bill's enactment, the legislation seemed to make it easier for Elkhart workers to support Malloy's resistance to the shutdown. It also rallied local support from unexpected sources. Elkhart County residents and leaders are politically conservative and protective of their "pro-business" environment. Although organized labor represented about 25% of all blue collar workers in the Elkhart area (roughly 20% higher than the national average), labor leaders there believe organized labor does not often receive official support.[5] However, Hiler's bill compelled the Mayor, the Chamber of Commerce and the local newspaper to endorse the union's fight.[6] This support was the first evidence that the issue of Section 936 could elicit the broad community support OCAW needed to take on AHP.

Union Support

Malloy needed also to convince members of her own union that the fight was worthwhile and carried little risk. Local unionists at Whitehall-Elkhart were not historically militant and thus were unaccustomed to fighting with AHP on any matter. Hiler's legislation shifted the blame from AHP and couched the struggle in terms more palatable to members reluctant even to identify themselves as union members. Hiler's bill allowed them to argue that this fight was not about high union wages or a dying industry attempting to survive. This fight was about a fundamental problem in the United States tax code, one that could affect nonunion as well as union jobs.[7]

The bill's most pivotal effect, however, was in drafting the attention and support of the OCAW International Union (OCAW-IU). The six hundred or so OCAW pharmaceutical workers in Elkhart didn't have much of a voice in the Denver international headquarters prior to 1990. There was virtually no history of labor-management trouble in Elkhart and thus little reason for the international union to be involved there outside of contract negotiations. When AHP's shutdown plans were revealed in the April contract negotiations, Malloy tried to enlist assistance from OCAW-IU for the Whitehall campaign. Her entreaties fell on deaf ears and she was told a fight would be futile because AHP would not change its decision.

There was, in fact, plenty of precedent for OCAW-IU's pessimism regarding the closure. OCAW had lost 2,100 members to AHP shutdowns and decertifications over the previous ten years. Locals 7-515 and 7-838 were OCAW's last remaining members employed by AHP. Likewise, OCAW-IU had reason to be pessimistic about reforming Section 936. OCAW-IU leaders and local officials had complained among themselves for years about Section 936 and the growing number of pharmaceutical plants in Puerto Rico, but had resigned hope for ever changing the law. When Malloy appeared before OCAW-IU leaders at a June 1990 Drug and Cosmetic Council meeting with a House bill in hand, she had instant credibility and so did her campaign to keep Whitehall open. The Hiler bill was proof of Malloy's initiative and commitment, important because she was nearly unknown to most OCAW-IU leaders. The bill also tapped into the union's pent-up frustration over the tax law and catalyzed OCAW-IU action on the Whitehall closure.

With OCAW-IU on board the union began to develop and implement a coherent campaign plan. They built on the opportunities provided by the Hiler bill and their tactics eventually evolved into an effective legalistic strategy. OCAW filed eight unfair labor practices charges against AHP before the National Labor Relations Board (NLRB). Later, OCAW filed three federal lawsuits, two under the Racketeer Influenced/Corrupt Organizations (RICO) Act and one under the Worker Adjustment and Retraining Notification (WARN) Act. It also filed a complaint with the Equal Employment Opportunity Commission (EEOC). Concurrently, OCAW enlisted additional Congressional support to amend Section 936.

This chapter first categorizes each of the union's maneuvers as either judicial or legislative then details the action and discusses the relevance of each to the union's overall goal of keeping the plant open. The legal actions are outlined first. Then, as a preface to the analysis of legislative actions, a brief history of Section 936 is provided. After all the actions have been outlined, the discussion details the outcome of each and summarizes the interconnections and countervailing influences among them, focusing on why certain maneuvers "worked" while others did not. Finally, the chapter evaluates the union's judicial and legislative strategy in an historical context.

TAKING THE BATTLE TO THE COURTS

Malloy thought U.S. organized labor naturally would get behind Hiler's bill and that, at the very least, OCAW could count on support from labor's reliable allies in Congress. Unfortunately for OCAW, labor's concerns over the political ramifications of supporting a Republican-sponsored labor bill eclipsed their concerns about stopping "runaway" plants. Hiler was a Republican and organized labor had thrown its support behind Hiler's Democratic opponent, Timothy Roemer.[8] Thus, the AFL-CIO did not support the passage of

Hiler's bill and the absence of this fundamental endorsement made it difficult to find co-sponsors for the legislation, even among labor's supporters. Ultimately, Hiler collected 29 co-sponsors in the summer and fall of 1990 but even this modest beginning was lost when Hiler was defeated in November of that year.

Nevertheless, OCAW-IU was fully committed to averting the plant closing by then. In July, OCAW's president, Joseph Misbrenner, assigned Richard Leonard to the Whitehall situation. Leonard was OCAW-IU's special projects director and was the union's resident "corporate campaign" strategist. Malloy already had the "campaign" well underway by this point but Leonard brought with him the experience of other OCAW corporate campaigns and the financial and organizational resources of the international union. This additional support proved to be critical in taking the campaign beyond November, when Hiler's bill languished in the wake of his election defeat.

Leonard immediately established a sophisticated media capability, which is examined in Chapter Three. His contacts in this arena led to the development of ties to interested parties in Puerto Rico. These contacts proved to be pivotal as the union's judicial strategy took shape. In the meantime, in Elkhart, local union leaders were busy filing unfair labor practices charges against Whitehall managers.

Unfair Labor Practices

Prior to 1990, neither Local 7-515 nor Local 7-838 made a habit of filing unfair labor practice charges with the National Labor Relations Board (NLRB) against Whitehall managers. In fact, in the five years prior to 1990, only three charges were filed and all of these were resolved before the cases were tried.[9] In the summer and fall of 1990, however, the company began to take a tougher line with the union and it responded by filing NLRB charges. In all, OCAW filed eight unfair labor practices charges between October 11, 1990 and December 12, 1990.

The NLRB charges were important to the union's campaign for a number of reasons. First, they helped maintain internal support among union members for the fight to keep the plant open. AHP delivered the official plant shutdown notification on October 1, 1990[10] and began laying off workers immediately; union leaders faced declining motivation and morale among their members. The official closure announcement and the layoffs made the shutdown real and imminent. The NLRB charges gave workers a tangible alternative to hang their hopes on, a sense they were fighting back, even if the chances for preventing the closure through a Board hearing were unlikely. They also showed workers that their fight would not be limited to demonstrations and rallies.

Second, the NLRB charges kept the Whitehall story in the local news. Inasmuch as OCAW's charges had merit, the union primarily intended them as political heat and to demonstrate in a public forum a pattern of "lawless" behavior by AHP. The local publicity about the NLRB charges kept pressure on Whitehall managers and demonstrated union resolve in the fight to keep Whitehall open.

Finally, the NLRB charges bought the union some time while it searched for AHP's Achilles' heel. OCAW leaders knew the Section 936 reform effort in Congress would not avert the Whitehall plant closure, especially since they would have to start over after Hiler's defeat. Hiler's bill had been a red flag that mobilized the pharmaceutical and Puerto Rican lobbies. For example, the Pharmaceutical Manufacturers Association (PMA) and several prominent Puerto Ricans contributed to Hiler's defeat that November by way of significant financial support for his opponent, Timothy Roemer.[11] In light of the powerful opposition, OCAW knew that a battle over Section 936 would be lengthy at best, and that it needed to find a more immediate and promising course of action. The NLRB charges were effective in this regard but were primarily defensive legal maneuvers, not the preeminent legal strategy OCAW soon developed to challenge AHP's decision to close Whitehall.

The first Board charge, filed on October 11, 1990 accused Whitehall of denying Malloy access to the plant as president of the union.[12] In September 1990, OCAW had made Malloy an "international representative" so she could devote herself full-time to the shutdown campaign.[13] Under the terms of the union contract, Whitehall granted Malloy a leave of absence from her regular job at the plant. In so doing, the company refused to recognize her any longer as president of the local union. It required she conduct her union business in the company's personnel office and only with permission from the company to be there.[14] The company's policy very effectively limited Malloy's direct access to OCAW members in the plant throughout the campaign. AHP's action proved to be an astute defensive move. The company identified Malloy as a significant threat and seized upon the opportunity of her leave of absence to preclude her influence in the plant. Malloy managed to find ways around this obstacle, nevertheless, and maintained some of her influence inside the plant in spite of Whitehall's limits on her access.

On October 31, 1990, OCAW filed two more charges against Whitehall.[15] One alleged Whitehall threatened to withhold benefits to grievance committee members. The second charged the company with failing to engage in a bargaining session with the union regarding its decision to close the Whitehall facility. The union charged that the company was obliged to provide the union information regarding its decision to close the Elkhart facility. OCAW hoped that a favorable ruling on this matter would result in a Board order to the company to engage in decision bargaining which could require it to turn over information regarding its decision to close Whitehall. OCAW wanted this official and public forum to make its point that the tax breaks in Puerto Rico were so lucrative that nothing the union could offer in terms of wage and benefit concessions could match them. . A decision bargaining session would not only delay the plant's closure but it could provide the union information with which it could attack AHP further.

OCAW filed three more charges on November 16, 1990.[16] The first complaint related to Malloy's initial charge that Whitehall interfered with her ability to conduct her duties as president of the local union. The second charged that a company vice-president threatened two union members with a loss of benefits or early closure if Malloy did not "shut her mouth." The third charged the company with retaliatory layoffs in response to an appearance at the plant by satirical documentary film producer, Michael Moore.

The last of the eight charges was filed on December 12. The union alleged that the company refused to bargain over the effects of the plant closing and also refused to provide the union information it needed to conduct such a bargaining session.[17]

Like the decision bargaining charge, this charge of failing to bargain over the effects of the plant closure was strategically critical. It established a minimum position for the union; union leaders knew that if all else failed, they had to have an opportunity to bargain for a better severance package than the one they had established in the April contract talks. Moreover, they hoped an effects session would force the company to share information with the union which might be helpful in its campaign.

On December 24 and 31, 1990, the Region 25 Director of the NLRB, William T. Little, announced the NLRB would prosecute AHP on five of the eight charges filed by OCAW. OCAW characterized the NLRB's filings as a "preliminary finding of guilt" and raised hopes further by stating that the union would seek to have the NLRB enjoin AHP from closing Whitehall.[18] The Board subsequently issued a consolidated complaint on January 31, 1991, including two additional charges, bringing the total to seven that would be prosecuted.

Little rejected OCAW's first complaint concerning Malloy's access to the plant on the grounds that it was not an NLRA violation to be decided by the NLRB but was a contractual matter subject to grievance arbitration.[19] OCAW appealed this ruling to the General Counsel of the NLRB who subsequently reversed the decision of the Regional Director and issued a complaint on March 29, 1991, bringing to eight the number of complaints consolidated and issued by the NLRB on OCAW's behalf.[20] Little scheduled the hearings for April 22, 1991. In the meantime, OCAW closed in on the adjudicative angle that would be the foundation of its battle in the courts.

The Puerto Rico "Hook"

Chicago Tribune business reporter, Merrill Goozner, and *Employment & Training Reporter* correspondent, Anne Mytych-DelPonte unwittingly provided OCAW with the legal hook the union believed it needed to attack AHP on grounds related to Section 936. OCAW had its campaign watchword in Section 936 but it lacked a concrete link between it, the Whitehall closing and AHP's new plant in Guayama, Puerto Rico. In an article on September 27, 1990, Goozner reported on the Whitehall situation in Elkhart and on Hiler's bill before Congress. For the Puerto Rican perspective, Goozner turned to the Puerto Rico USA Foundation (PRUSA), a coalition of 70 major U.S. firms with operations in Puerto Rico. In the last sentence of the article, Goozner quoted Peter Holmes, a consultant for the Foundation,

> We don't think the Hiler bill is necessary. Puerto Rican statutes provide that companies that establish operations there may not do so at the expense of jobs on the mainland.[21]

Mytych-DelPonte, for a story to be published in November, followed up on the Puerto Rican statutes mentioned in Goozner's story, and learned about the Puerto Rican Tax Incentives Act (PRTIA) provision to which Holmes referred. The provision states that the Governor of Puerto Rico may refuse an application for local tax benefits if

> ...the establishment of the unit for which exemption is sought would substantially and adversely affect the employees of an enterprise under related control operating in any state of the United States.[22]

Also, in the application for incentives under this tax provision, the corporate applicant must

> Indicate whether the establishment of applicant's proposed industrial unit in Puerto Rico will substantially and adversely affect the employees of an [sic] related control operation in any state of United States.[23]

In conversations with Malloy for her article, Mytych-DelPonte asked Malloy about the Puerto Rican statute. Malloy told her they were unaware of the specific provision and had overlooked the *Tribune's* reference to it.[24] Union leaders believed the statutes were clearly relevant to their campaign and they immediately set out to obtain a copy of them and of AHP's tax exemption application.

Fomento, Puerto Rico's economic development office in charge of administering tax exemption applications, refused to provide OCAW a copy of AHP's tax exemption application on the grounds that it contained confidential company information. OCAW argued the applications were public since they were filed in order to receive taxpayer-subsidized benefits. The union convinced Congressman Hiler to request the documents on its behalf, but he, too, was unable to obtain them perhaps owing to his "lame-duck" status following the November election defeat.

OCAW Goes to Puerto Rico

The reaction to Hiler's Section 936 reform bill by the Puerto Rico and pharmaceutical lobbies already had revealed to OCAW the extent of the opposition they faced on this issue. However, if Leonard and Malloy had any lingering doubts as to the overriding importance of Section 936 to these interest groups, they were vanquished by Fomento's apparent stonewalling on the issue of AHP's tax exemption application. The unionists believed they were on to something, and by

December, Malloy and Leonard were in Puerto Rico to find out what it was.

Prior to their trip, the union sent an "undercover investigator," Carlos Santiago, to investigate AHP's Guayama operation.[25] Santiago, a Puerto Rico academic who was then a visiting professor on the mainland, grew up in Guayama and knew the plant manager at AHP's facility there. Santiago obtained a tour of the plant and OCAW used the information he provided to allege that this "undercover investigator" had found evidence which showed that "AHP [was] moving products from Elkhart to Puerto Rico line by line."[26]

This information was interesting but irrelevant in terms of a lawsuit unless the union could show that moving a mainland plant to Puerto Rico was illegal. By now, OCAW was familiar with the PRTIA application procedure and believed AHP's application could be the keystone to a legal action against the company. Leonard and Malloy hoped an in-person request would be more successful than were their previous correspondences to obtain a copy of the application. OCAW's pursuit of AHP's application took them to, among others, Antonio Colorado, then Puerto Rico's Secretary of State; Alfredo Salazar, Fomento Administrator; and Sylvia Matos Pons, Director of Puerto Rico's Industrial Tax Exemption Office. Fomento again denied OCAW's request for a copy of AHP's application but did allow Malloy and Leonard to read AHP's response to Question 28 regarding mainland employment effects.

Malloy and Leonard had a broader agenda in traveling to Puerto Rico. Through their association with Santiago, the union had become familiar with the Puerto Rico power structure and political situation. Santiago put OCAW leaders in touch with Puerto Rico attorney Enrique Colón Santana prior to their trip to the island. According to OCAW, Colón Santana had begun to enlist support from a variety of island sources, including independence and statehood advocates and organized labor leaders. Thus, Malloy and Leonard's trip to Puerto Rico was an opportunity not only to find out about AHP's exemption application, but also to shore up this support from reform-minded Puerto Ricans.

OCAW made its presence in Puerto Rico known by arranging for interviews with the city editor of and several journalists for the island's primary English-language newspaper, *The San Juan Star*. Leonard and Malloy also met with Puerto Rico's Secretary of Labor,

President of the House of Representatives, and former Governor and leader of the New Progressive (pro-statehood) Party (PNP). Finally, they met with several key organized labor advocates and statehood and independence supporters, including Luis Costas-Elena, a former advisor to the PNP; an economic advisor to the Independence Party (PIP), and the Chairman of one of Puerto Rico's labor umbrella organizations, Comite de Organizaciones Sindicales.

During this visit, OCAW enjoyed extraordinary access to some of Puerto Rico's most powerful and influential individuals. OCAW's legislative reform effort was a threat to Section 936 and thus to the island's status quo. Even if OCAW's bill in the House stood little chance of becoming law, Puerto Rico leaders seemed to take the possibility seriously. They also expressed concern about OCAW's persistence on the matter of AHP's tax exemption application. Antonio Colorado complained that cases like Whitehall "create an image that, even though it's not true, is bad for us. It creates a problem."[27] The union's publicity campaign was well under way on the mainland and it was beginning to make headlines in the Puerto Rico press. Leonard assailed Fomento administrators for refusing to provide OCAW and Hiler with copies of AHP's exemption application, "we've tried going through the front door in Puerto Rico, but we haven't had any luck with Fomento."[28] OCAW's allusion to an alternative "back-door" approach served notice that its campaign would eventually encompass Puerto Rico officials. Thus, when union leaders arrived in December, they already had established considerable political leverage and many doors opened to them.

OCAW made the most of its trip to Puerto Rico by cultivating support from a wide variety of interest groups. The union forged alliances with and among individuals and interest groups who had no particular interest in the workers in Elkhart but whose political agendas paralleled OCAW's goals. OCAW's views about the Puerto Rico political situation were informed largely by Colón-Santana and he led OCAW leaders to other island groups that had an interest in the union's effort. OCAW's allies in Puerto Rico all wanted a fundamental economic redirection away from the island's dependence on Section 936; some advocated statehood as the answer, others independence. Inasmuch as their approaches differed, these interest groups shared a common enemy in Section 936. OCAW's attack on the tax law and those who administered it united them and this *de facto* coalition of disparate yet powerful interests endowed the Whitehall campaign with broad significance and consequently enabled OCAW's lawsuits in Puerto Rico.

OCAW Files RICO Suit

In addition to providing information about AHP's Guayama facility, Carlos Santiago put OCAW in touch with Enrique Colón Santana, a Puerto Rico attorney who had long involved himself with causes on behalf of the poor and disenfranchised in Puerto Rico. Colón Santana, had some experience in RICO cases and helped arrange for OCAW's meetings in Puerto Rico. He also helped OCAW shape its legal strategy and convinced the union it had the grounds for a lawsuit under the federal RICO statute. Within six weeks after returning from Puerto Rico, OCAW filed a $100 million RICO suit (RICO I) with the federal court in San Juan. The suit charged both AHP and Puerto Rico officials with violations of this federal statute.

The trip to Puerto Rico yielded information which would serve as the foundation of the union's legal allegations against the company. Most important was AHP's tax grant application. OCAW interpreted AHP's negative response to question 28 as evidence that the company had certified that its Guayama operation would not cause any mainland job losses. Also the union alleged that AHP fraudulently included its Guayama plant under the tax exempt status of "a pre-existing but unrelated AHP subsidiary in Guayama" in order to claim tax exemptions on products for which it had not yet attained official tax exempt status.[29] (AHP had an Ayerst-Wyeth plant in Guayama prior to building the Whitehall facility.) OCAW claimed this "scheme" provided AHP the opportunity to hide the movement of equipment and intangibles to its new Guayama facility and illegally shelter millions of dollars in profits.

OCAW also clarified Puerto Rico's legal obligations for conferring Section 936 status on a company. The Puerto Rico Tax Incentives Act of 1987 (PRTIA) mandated the Governor to "revoke any exemption granted under this Act if it was obtained by false or fraudulent representations concerning the nature of the eligible business."[30] OCAW learned that no Governor had ever revoked a tax exemption and that no company's Section 936 status had ever been challenged on those grounds. OCAW's meetings in Puerto Rico helped union leaders sort out who specifically was responsible for administering Puerto Rico's tax incentives and thus who might be culpable in terms of a lawsuit.

The mandatory revocation clause of the PRTIA would seem to be the most obvious and direct adjudicative measure OCAW could have pursued in its attempt to keep open the Whitehall-Elkhart plant. If the Governor was forced to revoke AHP's tax exemption, AHP arguably could have reconsidered producing in Guayama and this may have forestalled the plant's closure for the immediate future. In fact, Fomento administrators offered to hold an administrative hearing on AHP's application, but the union turned down the offer.[31] By choosing not to pursue this course of action, OCAW clearly thought they had more to gain by impugning AHP and the Puerto Rico government as "racketeers" and charging them with Section 936 fraud. Also, the union had no confidence in a hearing and believed it would only delay progress on averting the shutdown. Moreover, a hearing could hurt its chances for prevailing in a legal action if the union were forced by the hearing process to reveal its alleged "runaway" evidence.

RICO I's fundamental assertion was that AHP decided in 1986 to build the plant in Guayama, close the plant in Elkhart, and transfer the Elkhart jobs to Guayama. The complaint alleged that this transfer of jobs was illegal and that it was accomplished through a pattern of racketeering behavior by American Home Products, Ayerst-Wyeth Pharmaceuticals (an AHP subsidiary), and Whitehall Laboratories in conspiracy with Antonio J. Colorado (Puerto Rico's Secretary of State), Rafael Hernandez Colon (Governor of Puerto Rico),and Sylvia Matos (Head of Puerto Rico's Industrial Tax Exemption Office). Specifically, as a way of establishing a pattern of illegal activity, the complaint alleged violations of not only RICO, but also of PRTIA, Section 936, Puerto Rico corporation laws, the U.S. Department of Labor Jobs Training Partnership Act (JTPA)[32], and U.S. Department of Commerce Economic Development Agency regulations. OCAW filed the suit on January 22, 1991 in the U.S. District Court for the District of Puerto Rico.[33]

AHP countered that the decision to close Whitehall-Elkhart had nothing to do with its decision to build the Guayama facility. AHP explained that it made the decision to build Guayama in 1986 when it was short on capacity and needed to bring Advil production in-house. (Prior to Guayama, Advil was produced under contract by a British pharmaceutical manufacturer, Boots, Ltd.) The company said it decided to close Whitehall-Elkhart four years later when it was faced with overcapacity due to its acquisition of A.H. Robins in 1989 and that the tax benefits of Section 936 did not factor at all into its decision to close Elkhart. Also, AHP strenuously objected the union's characterization of its Whitehall closure as a "runaway" and argued that neither the union nor anyone else could show a direct, one-to-one transfer of jobs from Whitehall to its Puerto Rico operation.

OCAW's primary allegation was that AHP committed fraud on its tax exemption application. OCAW claimed the Puerto Rico government permitted the fraud by choosing not to verify AHP's claim that the Guayama plant would have no adverse mainland employment effects. In essence, the union alleged AHP's action and the Puerto Ricans' unwillingness to act was a corrupt conspiracy. This reasoning formed the theoretical basis for the union's lawsuit. This argument may have been legitimate from a theoretical standpoint and may have represented the truth of the situation, however, the legal argumentation of the RICO I complaint was weak and seemed ripe for dismissal.

Legal scholars expert in RICO litigation would have no trouble pointing out the problems with OCAW's RICO I complaint, but such an exercise is beyond the scope of this analysis. It must be said, however, that cases with significantly more RICO substance than this one have been summarily dismissed by the courts both prior and subsequent to OCAW's complaint. Indeed, OCAW leaders knew a lawsuit based on RICO was a long shot but thought they had enough of a case to warrant discovery. They also hoped it would pay off in political terms, if not in the courtroom.

OCAW's suit did present compelling information, whether or not it was relevant in terms of RICO. In his trip to Puerto Rico, OCAW's "undercover investigator" saw evidence which, together with information from Local 7-515, convinced OCAW leaders that at least one packaging line had been transferred directly from Elkhart to Puerto Rico. In RICO I, the union outlined its equipment transfer allegation in detail. Additionally, RICO I alleged that AHP received tax benefits on production which was not officially exempt. This accusation raised the specter that AHP had manipulated Puerto Rico government officials and the union characterized these actions as fraudulent and illegal.

AHP attorneys characterized RICO I as misguided and filed a motion to dismiss it on February 25, 1991. AHP argued the plant closing situation should be characterized as a labor dispute involving "grievances arising out of collective bargaining"[34] to be resolved by the NLRB, not by the federal court. AHP went on to argue that, on the basis of the principles of federalism, the federal court had no business interfering in the administration of Puerto Rico tax law. Also, they argued, even if OCAW's allegations regarding Section 936, JTPA and EDA abuses were true (AHP denied that they were), individuals did not have a legal "right of action" to recover funds under these statutes, only the federal government did. AHP maintained that the union neither pled nor presented the statutory elements necessary to state a RICO claim and, even if they had, the union could show no injury flowing from such a violation.[35] AHP characterized OCAW's complaint as simply "another vehicle in its public relations and political campaign" against the defendants.

Indeed, OCAW's RICO I complaint was long on political rhetoric and appears to have been written with a broader audience in mind. It made sweeping generalizations about Section 936 that seemed to serve the union's political agenda more than strengthen its legal arguments. OCAW leaders knew their complaint, from a legal standpoint, was on shaky ground. They attributed this only to a lack of access to evidence, however, and proceeded to devise ways by which they could obtain solid substantiation of their job transfer allegation.

Worker Adjustment and Retraining Notification Act (WARN) Lawsuit

In November 1990, OCAW had begun to consider suing AHP for violations of the Worker Adjustment and Retraining Notification (WARN) Act of 1988[36] after Whitehall officials suddenly laid off more workers than they had announced previously. OCAW initiated discussions with the Chicago firm of Despres, Schwartz and Geoghahan over the possibility of a WARN lawsuit. The union decided to proceed with the WARN allegation prior to its trip to Puerto Rico in December. It filed the WARN complaint on February 2, 1991 two weeks after it filed RICO I. Union leaders believed a WARN suit would be another opportunity to recover compensation for the workers. Later, however, as the RICO complaint took shape and its evidentiary shortcomings surfaced, the WARN suit took on additional meaning. It turned out to be another opportunity to obtain discovery into when AHP decided to build its Guayama plant and when it decided to close Whitehall-Elkhart.

The U.S. Congress enacted the Worker Adjustment and Retraining Notification Act in 1988 to require companies to give their employees advance notification of a business closing or mass layoff. In the few years since its enactment, WARN has proved to be largely impotent. It has many "exceptions" by which firms can avoid giving advance notice. Furthermore, even if a firm is found to have violated WARN statutes, the penalties for such violations are insignificant. Only about 125 complaints have been filed since 1988 when the law was enacted; the interpretation of the law is evolving.

The WARN Act basically requires firms with 100 or more employees to give 60 days' advance notification prior to a plant shutdown or mass layoff. The law also empowers the U.S. Department of Labor to "prescribe such regulations as may be necessary to carry out this Act."[37] OCAW filed suit against AHP on February 7, 1991 and alleged violations of both the WARN act and Department of Labor regulations that govern it.

Specifically, OCAW argued AHP was required to give each individual employee notice 60 days in advance of his or her actual termination date. AHP argued it had given all the Whitehall workers thirteen months' advance notice of its planned November 1, 1991 shutdown date, six times the notice required by law. The union argued the blanket notice was insufficient and ambiguous and frustrated the intent of the WARN Act, "an employee who simply knows he will be terminated...at some point in a 12-month period can be taken by surprise as to his actual termination date, and deprived of the ability to make an appropriate plan for adjustment or retraining."[38] OCAW Local 7-515 filed the complaint in the United States District Court for the Northern District of Indiana, South Bend.

Alleging WARN violations based on this specificity of notice requirement was a novel legal approach but one that ultimately failed.[39] Although AHP prevailed in the end, the lawsuit proved to be of enormous benefit to the union in the course of its campaign against the company. OCAW's WARN lawsuit was not a direct attempt to keep the plant open. In fact, WARN specifically prohibits the federal court from enjoining a plant closing or a mass layoff as a legal remedy for violations of the act.[40] Moreover, OCAW did not expect an offer to settle the case since AHP's risk and cost to defend itself was relatively low, even if the federal court ruled in the union's favor. OCAW's WARN suit was primarily a strategic maneuver; although a WARN victory payout would have been inconsequential to AHP, for individual workers the back pay award would have been substantial. Also, the union hoped to open a second line of discovery. Meanwhile, in the same week OCAW filed WARN charges, the NLRB scheduled the hearings on OCAW's unfair labor practices charges against Whitehall to begin in April.

NLRB Hearings

The NLRB hearings originally were set to begin on April 22, 1991. In early April, the NLRB convinced OCAW to withdraw its eighth charge regarding whether AHP had an obligation to bargain over its decision to close the Whitehall plant and sent it to arbitration. The NLRB decided AHP was not obligated under federal labor law to negotiate with the union regarding the decision to close the plant. OCAW's withdrawal represented a significant victory for AHP because it eliminated the possibility that the NLRB hearings would in any way delay the plant's closure planned for November of that year. Also it closed off one opportunity for OCAW to gain access to information it could use against the company.

When the April 22 hearing arrived, the Board attorneys encouraged the parties to resolve the issues out of court in a pre-hearing conference. This settlement attempt failed and the Board reset the hearing date for April 29. On this date, the parties met again to try to reach a settlement but after three weeks of meetings, failed to resolve any of the issues. The Board rescheduled the hearings for June.

U.S. Department of Labor administrative law judge John West began the hearings on June 4, 1991 in Elkhart, Indiana and they lasted five days. Local newspapers reported that the tone of the hearings was acrimonious and the differences "extreme."[41] The company defendants denied the union's charges and said the union filed them only to embarrass AHP. The company claimed the charges were baseless and simply part of a campaign against them by the Denver-based international union. During the hearings, AHP accused the union of planning to sabotage a production line. The company also subpoenaed two union members caught going through the garbage of the LaPorte, Indiana law firm representing AHP in the NLRB proceedings.

NLRB attorneys prosecuted the charges against the company.[42] They argued the company had a contractual obligation and a legal obligation under the National Labor Relations Act to bargain over the effects of the closure. The company insisted they already had bargained over the effects of the closure during the April 1990 contract negotiations.[43]

On the matter regarding AHP's refusal to recognize Malloy as the local union president while she also was an international union representative, the NLRB attorneys produced a witness who had also held both positions at Whitehall. This witness testified he was never denied free access to the plant or recognition as the local union president.[44]

In post-hearing press conferences, both sides claimed victory. It would be over seven months, however, before the administrative law judge ruled on the charges—three months after the Whitehall plant closed its doors for good.

Discovery

As the company and the union attempted to reach settlement on the NLRB charges, Judge Miller, on May 14, 1991, ordered discovery to begin into the WARN allegations. Then, as the NLRB hearings proceeded in Elkhart, U.S. District Court Judge Jaime Pieras in Puerto Rico denied AHP's motion to dismiss OCAW's RICO complaint and ordered discovery to begin into the RICO allegations. Pieras issued his ruling on May 31, 1991 and stated that OCAW had "provided an outline of a general scheme to defraud with allegations that make it likely that the defendant used interstate mail or telecommunications facilities."[45]

The WARN and RICO discovery orders were serious blows to AHP and incredible opportunities for the union. Discovery would require AHP essentially to open its books and files to the union, now its bitter enemy. It was clear that OCAW would try to use the information it gained not only to strengthen its cases in the courts but also to fuel its public relations operation. Thus, AHP fought hard to restrict the documents available to the union, filing numerous motions throughout the summer of 1991 to reduce OCAW's access to its files.

Pieras denied or simply set aside AHP's motions and by the end of August 1991, over 100,000 pages of documents were in South Bend, Indiana and Guayama, Puerto Rico under the perusal of Leonard, Colon-Santana, and Malloy. By now, OCAW had dropped from RICO I allegations that the defendants also had violated Section 936, JTPA, EDA and PRTIA regulations and limited the complaint solely to violations of the RICO statute. AHP pointed out this backpedalling in a reply to the OCAW brief that excluded these ancillary charges. AHP saw this redirection as proof that OCAW's RICO complaint was weak and groundless. "The union, in short, is asking the court for permission to conduct a fishing expedition," charged AHP.[46] Pieras granted the expedition, hook, line and sinker.

Legal Counsel Fortification

As discovery in the WARN and RICO cases proceeded and AHP witnesses were deposed, OCAW leaders began to believe they were outgunned in terms of their legal representation in the RICO case. Legal costs were mounting because Colon-Santana charged the union by the hour rather than on a contingency basis. OCAW also started to believe they had the grounds for a much larger class-action suit under RICO but could not afford to bring a second suit on an hours-worked basis. OCAW contacted Alan Kanner, an attorney in Philadelphia who had established a reputation for winning substantial settlements in suits against large corporations on behalf of "little guy" clients.

In the 1980's, Kanner won settlements against the Three Mile Island utilities, Ralston Purina, ChemLawn, Equitable Life Assurance Society, and Amoco Corporation. Also, he represented 14,000 Owens-Corning Fiberglas Corp. workers who lost their jobs after that firm's expensive defense against a takeover by Wickes Cos. U.S labor leaders took notice of Kanner in the Wickes case and soon thereafter Kanner began to represent laid-off union workers in class-action suits against their former employers.[47] In 1990, Kanner also filed a novel racketeering suit against a major pharmaceutical company, Johnson & Johnson, on behalf of two former employees. Thus, when OCAW decided to strengthen its legal team, Kanner's credentials made him the clear choice. Kanner and OCAW began discussions in October 1991.

The plant closed on schedule on November 1, 1991. In the preceding months, when the pace of layoffs increased and equipment was moved out of the plant, OCAW leaders knew they would not be able to forestall the plant closing and narrowed their strategy then to maximizing severance compensation to the Whitehall workers. OCAW leaders knew they had to be able to keep up with and respond adequately to the AHP and Commonwealth attorneys' motions in order to continue the lawsuit. The discovery process was a critical window of opportunity that could be shut if the union was unable to continue to demonstrate to the court the legal substance of its case. By this time, the RICO lawsuit was the essence of OCAW's pressure on AHP. There was little hope for effecting a big settlement for the workers without the RICO suit. Even if the NLRB administrative law judge eventually were to rule that AHP must conduct effects bargaining and reexamine the workers' severance payments, the union would have little leverage to influence the size of AHP's offer without the threat of the RICO suit behind it. OCAW needed the resources and experience of an Alan Kanner to keep the RICO suit going.

Kanner expressed an interest in the case and a willingness to take it on a contingency basis but initially would not commit. He continued to stall through the end of the year and up to February 3, 1992 when Judge Pieras ordered the trial for RICO I to begin on March 30. Suddenly, Kanner was on board and three weeks later, on February 26, 1992, he filed a new $1 billion class action RICO suit against AHP and the Commonwealth defendents (RICO II).

RICO II: Broadening the Allegations

RICO II[48] differed from the first RICO suit in several ways. First, RICO II was a class action suit and included 1,400 former employees from not only the Whitehall Laboratories facility in Elkhart but also from a Wyeth-Ayerst Laboratories plant in Great Valley, Pennsylvania. Wyeth-Ayerst is a division of American Home Products Corp. and manufactured ethical and over-the-counter pharmaceuticals at Great Valley, PA, Rouses Point, NY and other locations. The Great Valley workers included in the class were not members of OCAW or any other union. The complaint also identified two other AHP production facilities OCAW claimed suffered job losses as a result of the opening of the Guayama facility. Next, RICO II sued for one billion dollars to compensate the class and punish the defendants. RICO I called for compensation in the amount of $100 million.

RICO II benefited enormously from the discovery documents and depositions available to OCAW as a result of RICO I and its WARN suit. RICO II set forth, in much greater detail and with what seemed to be significantly more substantiation, the defendants' "scheme to defraud."[49] OCAW alleged that documents obtained in the RICO I discovery indicated that AHP had transferred production from other mainland plants to its Guayama facility. RICO II quoted numerous reports and correspondences which OCAW said showed the Great Valley plant lost production to Puerto Rico. It pointed out that some of the most incriminating correspondence and documentation regarding a direct transfer of production from the states to Puerto Rico was from plants other than Whitehall-Elkhart.

For example, OCAW cited a document entitled, "Transfer of Products to AWPI: Update" which summarized "the entire transfer process by grant number and point[ed] to additional transfers taking place throughout 1989, 1990 and 1991 from the Great Valley site" to the Ayerst-Wyeth Pharmaceutical (AWPI) plant in Guayama.[50] Similarly, a 1986 AHP proposal for expanding the Guayama facility stated, "both Ayerst and Wyeth are planning to transfer several other products to Puerto Rico all of which require manufacturing techniques not now existing at AWPI" and listed ethical pharmaceuticals then manufactured at the Rouses Point, NY production facility.[51]

In order to characterize these other transfers as illegal under RICO, OCAW had to include the workers from the other affected plants in its case and argue they also were hurt by the defendants' actions. OCAW convinced a number of former Great Valley workers to join the class. OCAW was unable, however, to draft the support of laid-off workers from AHP facilities in Rouses Point, NY and Hammonton, NJ. At the time, AHP was channeling new production lines to both Rouses Point and Hammonton and workers there believed they would jeopardize this trend by joining in OCAW's legal action. Moreover, as Chapter Four discusses, some unionists at Rouses Point viewed OCAW as a renegade union and did not want to associate themselves with an OCAW attack of any kind. OCAW made the case anyway that production was transferred directly from Hammonton and Rouses Point to Guayama, even without the explicit support of the workers there. (It is notable that because of the way OCAW defined the RICO "class," Rouses Point workers shared in the $24 million settlement despite their lack of support.) Thus, RICO II significantly broadened OCAW's legal attack on AHP. It linked transfers from four mainland plants to the Guayama facility and, in effect, called into question the legality of AHP's entire productive capacity in Puerto Rico.

RICO II also outlined more convincingly the role of the Puerto Rico government defendants in the "scheme to defraud." In order for the RICO allegations to stand, the plaintiffs had to prove, among other requirements, that an "enterprise" existed to conduct and facilitate racketeering activities. RICO II argued that, together, the AHP defendants and the Puerto Rico defendants comprised the enterprise in this situation and as such "calculated to deceive and defraud ...so as to enrich each defendant."[52] OCAW characterized the Puerto Rico officials as obsequieous political opportunists who were so eager for the AHP jobs that they neglected their oversight responsiblities and even rewrote tax laws to facilitate the firm's illegal relocation of jobs to Puerto Rico. OCAW quoted from an AHP letter to Antonio Colorado, which included a draft of proposed legislation entitled, "Proposed Wording for New Tax Incentives Act." OCAW went on to point out that the final legislation "precisely reflect[ed]" AHP's suggested revisions.[53]

RICO II yielded OCAW distinct advantages. The potential payoff was bigger, the factual allegations were better substantiated, and the RICO violations were more adequately pled. By filing a separate suit, Kanner was the lead counsel and as such was the face of the lawsuit. AHP attorneys viewed Kanner as more aggressive than his predecessor and this opinion served the interests of the union. RICO II also offered significant public relations opportunities, as Chapter Three discusses, and helped escalate the pressure on AHP.

RICO II was not without risks, however. A new suit opened up a new set of opportunities upon which AHP could base motions to dismiss the complaint. AHP fought vigorously, for example, to prevent the "certification of the class." AHP argued that the former employees named in OCAW's complaint did not comprise a legitimate "class" of plaintiffs because they were not numerous enough and their claims were neither similar nor typical. Pieras held a separate hearing on the matter, and in spite of the defendants' strenuous opposition, the judge ruled in the union's favor. Also, by involving four plants in the complaint, OCAW had to prove the causal link between an AHP action and job losses for each of the four plants. In RICO I, it only had to prove the Elkhart-to-Guayama link. Nevertheless, as Judge Pieras continued to rule in the union's favor or not rule at all on various AHP motions, the advantages to the union of the second RICO suit quickly outweighed the risks.

Initially, sources close to the case predicted that Judge Pieras would not join the two RICO complaints.[54] On April 21, 1992, however, Pieras consolidated the two complaints. This was another break for the union because the trial date for RICO I already had been set. The consolidation of the two meant it was likely that the judge would continue apace to push the cases toward trial.

By the spring of 1992, OCAW's battle in the courts showed remarkable promise. The NLRB charges and the WARN suit appeared to be near resolution and virtually all the momentum in the RICO suits favored the union. At the same time, on Capitol Hill, legislation introduced in 1991 which was designed to gut Section 936 was making its way through the U.S. House of Representatives.

TAKING THE FIGHT TO CAPITOL HILL

OCAW's struggle to reform Section 936 of the U.S. Internal Revenue Code began with Hiler's *American Jobs Stability Act of 1990* and ended three and a half years later when the U.S. Congress enacted the *Omnibus Budget Reconciliation Act (OBRA) of 1993*. Although OCAW began the reform effort in support of its campaign to keep Whitehall open, the union's goals and strategies evolved as the circumstances of its campaign changed. Three distinct phases characterize OCAW's fight on Capitol Hill. The first phase ended when Hiler was defeated in the November 1990 Congressional election. The second ended when the union and the company reached a settlement in the RICO suits. The final phase culminated in the passage of the OBRA, wherein Congress significantly cut back Section 936 benefits.

The first phase had at its center the Hiler bill and its emphasis on denying Section 936 tax benefits to "relocated business operations", or as the union preferred to call them, "runaways." Although this legislative effort was OCAW's first action in the Whitehall campaign, Section 936 reform was not, at this point, the union's primary goal. OCAW wanted to avert the Whitehall plant closing, then failing that, it sought to maximize severance compensation for laid-off Whitehall workers. In April 1990, when AHP signalled it probably would close Whitehall, Malloy searched frantically for any and all means to keep the jobs in Elkhart. Malloy thought Whitehall was a "runaway" to Puerto Rico impelled by the Section 936 tax break. She sought help from Hiler to save the Elkhart jobs and he was willing to go after the tax provision legislatively. She gladly accepted his help and tax reform proved to be the most powerful strategy they could have chosen anyway. OCAW *began* the fight to reform Section 936 because it served the interests of their members at Whitehall-Elkhart.

OCAW *continued* its Section 936 reform bid after the plant closed in order to pressure AHP to offer a substantial severance package, either through a settlement of the lawsuits or an effects bargaining session. This change in objectives marked the beginning of the second phase of OCAW's legislative effort. Among all industries in Puerto Rico, pharmaceutical companies had the most to lose from a change in Section 936, thus OCAW's effort to reform it represented significant pressure on AHP. In this second phase, OCAW mounted a real and serious effort to cut back Section 936 because only a serious threat could pressure AHP to settle. OCAW garnered the support of a powerful Congressman on the House Ways and Means Committee and introduced legislation that would deny Section 936 benefits to companies that the Department of the Treasury determined were runaways from the mainland. That this reform proposal was a union tactic rather than its ultimate goal made it no less real a threat, however, as far as Section 936 proponents were concerned.

Some have argued that OCAW's role in the 1993 reform of Section 936 was merely coincidental and that the reform was bound to happen anyway. It is more accurate to say that the union used to its advantage, coincident political circumstances to define the Section 936 battle in terms that served its own particular purposes. While it is true that there were many other parties interested in amending Section 936, no other group so clearly articulated the problems of the tax incentive in terms that were meaningful to Americans and their representatives in Congress. One need only examine prior attempts to reform Section 936 in 1976, 1982 and 1986 to discern OCAW's influence on the 1993 reform effort. To this end, Section 936 must be understood in the broader context of tax incentives generally in the economic development history of Puerto Rico. It is impossible to understand how the union's third legislative drive brought about reform in 1993 without first knowing something of the history of Section 936 and other tax incentives regarding Puerto Rico.

Table 1 summarizes federal and Puerto Rico tax incentive legislation from 1900 to 1993. This table is skeletal by design and is meant to illustrate the evolution of the current tax incentive legislation and to synopsize Congressional and Puerto Rico activity on these matters over the years. It is in no way exhaustive or entirely

TABLE 1
Evolution of Tax Incentives Regarding Puerto Rico

Year	Legislation	Impact on Federal Tax Liability	Impact on Puerto Rico Tax Liability
1900	Foraker Act[a]	Individuals exempt	N/A
1913	U.S. Corporate Income Tax	Corporations taxed on income	Corporations taxed on income; rate same as federal rate
1917	Jones Act[b]	Corporations & individuals exempt	N/A
1921	Revenue Act[c]	Corporations exempt if 80% income from island & 50% from active business; tax-free repatriation of profits only if island assets liquidated	N/A
1947	Puerto Rico Industrial Incentives Act (PRIIA)[d]	N/A	Corporations 100% exempt to 1959, partially exempt to 1962
1948	Industrial Tax Exemption Act[e]	N/A	Amended PRIIA; denied tax exemption to runaway firms
1952	Federal Relations Act (referendum)[f]	N/A	Established Commonwealth status for Puerto Rico
1954	Puerto Rico Industrial Incentives Act[g]	N/A	Firms fully exempt for 10 years after operations begin
1963	Puerto Rico Industrial Incentives Act[h]	N/A	Full exemption for longer periods if located outside San Juan
1976	Tax Reform Act[i]	Created S936: tax free repatriation without liquidation of assets; changed exemption to a credit; required QPSII to be eligible for S936 status	N/A
1976	Puerto Rico P.L. 95, Act of June 1, 1976[j]	N/A	Established 10% tollgate tax

[a] C.145, 31 Stat. 77
[b] C.145, 39 Stat. 951
[c] C.136, 42 Stat. 227
[d] Act of December 5, 1947, no. 22, p.376.
[e] 13 Laws of Puerto Rico Annotated (L.P.R.A.) §§ 221-238
[f] Public Law 600
[g] 13 L.P.R.A. §§ 241-251
[h] 13 L.P.R.A. §§ 252-252j
[i] Public Law No. 94-455, 90 Stat. 1520
[j] 13 L.P.R.A. §§ 3144, 3231

TABLE 1
Evolution of Tax Incentives Regarding Puerto Rico

1978	Puerto Rico Industrial Incentives Act[k]	N/A	Allowed S936 corps. to reduce tollgate tax to 5% if they invested tax liability in P.R.; complete tax exemption replaced by diminishing scales; service industries now qualify for S936 status
1982	Tax Equity & Fiscal Responsibility Act (TEFRA)[l]	Intangibles taxable unless "significant business presence" (25% value added content & 65% labor content); active trade requirement raised to 65%	N/A
1983	Caribbean Basin Economic Recovery Act (CBERA)[m]	Enacted Caribbean Basin Initiative (CBI); CBI products duty-free to U.S. if 35% value-added in CBI countries including Puerto Rico	N/A
1986	Tax Reform Act[n]	Raised active trade requirement to 75%; allowed QPSII to be used to build plants in CBI countries (twin plant strategy); tightened intangibles income requirements; cut U.S. corporate tax rate from 52% to 46%	P.R. government committed to spend $100 million annually of S936 funds invested in P.R. on CBI development projects
1987	Puerto Rico Tax Incentives Act[o]	N/A	Tax exemption schedule changed to flat 90% for a minimum of 10 yrs.;exemption extensions at 75% for 10 more yrs.
1993	Omnibus Budget Reconciliation Act (OBRA)[p]	S936 exemption cut to 60% of income in 1994, 55% in 1995, 50 % in 1996, 45% in 1997, 40% in 1998 and after; OR firms may elect a wage-based credit (60% of wages & fringes)	N/A

[k] 13 L.P.R.A. §§ 255-255m
[l] Pub. L. No. 97-248, 96 Stat. 324
[m] Pub. L. No. 98-67, 97 Stat. 369
[n] Pub. L. No. 99-514, 100 Stat. 2085
[o] 13 L.P.R.A. §256
[p] Pub. L. No. 103-66, 107 Stat. 489

expositive; it is simply one version of the historical "big picture" of investment incentives regarding Puerto Rico. The following could be considered the narrative to that picture.

Origin of tax exempt status for individuals and corporations

Federal tax preferences for Puerto Rico date back to the Foraker Act of 1900. This law was was enacted within two years of the U.S. takeover of Puerto Rico from Spain in 1898 and temporarily codified Puerto Rico's political and economic relationship with the United States. Under the Foraker provisions, individuals in Puerto Rico paid no federal income taxes, and because there was no corporate income tax in the U.S. until 1913, neither did corporations. The Jones Act of 1917 permanently codified the federal personal income tax exemption for Puerto Ricans and extended it to corporations. However, U.S. corporations were still subject to taxation by the Puerto Rico government, whose rates were very close to the U.S. federal rate at that time.[55]

The Jones Act also granted Puerto Ricans U.S. citizenship but they remained otherwise politically unrepresented in the U.S. Congress due to the island's ambiguous status as an "unincorporated territory" rather than as a state of the United States. This lack of representation is the fundamental Constitutional explanation for why Puerto Rican individuals were (and still are) not subject to federal income taxation. It also helps to explain why the Jones Act initially exempted corporations from federal income taxation.

Origin of Section 936 and its centrality in Puerto Rico's economy

Section 936 had its origin in the Revenue Act of 1921 as Section 931. Congress enacted Section 931 to allow U.S. firms in U.S. possessions to operate free from federal income taxation. The law targeted firms in the Philippines (then a U.S. possession) and was intended to put them on an equal footing with their foreign competitors whose home governments allowed them to operate there tax-free also. The law covered companies in all U.S. possessions, including Puerto Rico. Section 931 departed, however, from the entirely tax-free environment afforded by the Jones Act. Firms could operate free of federal income taxation only if 80 percent of their gross income originated from the territory and at least 50 percent was derived from the "active" conduct of business (as opposed to "passive" income derived from financial investments). Also, U.S. parent corporations could not repatriate profits tax-free from their Puerto Rico subsidiaries unless they liquidated the assets that produced the profits. At this point, although Section 931-qualified "possessions corporations" paid no federal income taxes, they were required to pay the local Puerto Rico corporate income tax which was levied at roughly the same rate as the mainland corporate tax rate. The corporate tax picture on the island remained largely unchanged until 1947.

In the seven years just prior to 1947, Puerto Rico set into motion a very constructive political and economic period under the direction of the appointed governor, Rexford G. Tugwell, and the president of the Puerto Rico Senate, Luis Muñoz Marin.[56] Together, Tugwell, who had been appointed by President Franklin Roosevelt, and Muñoz Marin undertook their own New Deal for Puerto Rico which laid the foundation for a rapid and profound transformation of the island economy.[57]

The 1930's had been a violent and politically fractious period for Puerto Rico. The island was very poor and because of the inherent ambiguity of its status with regard to the United States, there was virtually no economic or political infrastructure in place to address the island's economic problems. The economy was based on export-oriented agriculture and most island inhabitants lived in poor, rural surroundings. Governor Tugwell and Muñoz Marin believed that industrialization would ameliorate Puerto Rico's poverty and unemployment. Thus in 1941, in the spirit of New-Deal, Keynesian economics, Tugwell and Muñoz Marin began to set up public corporations and state-financed industries that were to employ native skills and raw materials with the goal of modernizing and "injecting new life into the ailing economy of the island." The government set up various institutions including the Junta de Salario (Minimum Wage Board), the Autoridad de las Fuentes Fluviales (Water Resources Authority),and the Autoridad de Tierras (Land Authority). The most important government institutions set up in this time period were the Compania de Fomento (Development Company) and the Banco de Fomento (Development Bank). They directed the industrialization of the island in the period between 1941 and 1946 and established several public corporations including cement, glass, paper, pottery and shoe factories.

These factories floundered, however, while the U.S. Congress began to attack the island's new development policies as Socialist experiments. Congress' suspicions about Tugwell's intentions paved the way for granting Puerto Ricans the right to elect their own governor. These factors, combined with the persistence of extreme poverty and unemployment on the island, forced Puerto Rico leaders to change their development policy and dedicate their energies to attracting private U.S. capital to the island through the use of tax incentives. In spite of the specific policy failures, the institutional structure created during the Tugwell-Muñoz Marin years persisted.

In 1945 Muñoz Marin placed Teodoro Moscoso in charge of the island's industrialization program. In 1947, Moscoso introduced his now-famous "Operation Bootstrap" development program to industrialize the island economy. The cornerstone of Operation Bootstrap was Puerto Rico's Industrial Incentive Act (PRIIA) of 1947 which completely exempted qualifying firms from insular taxation. This incentive combined with the federal tax holiday of Section 931 provided U.S. firms with an essentially tax-free domestic production location. In 1950, the government established the Administración de Fomento Económico (Economic Development Administration) to promote the island's tax benefits to mainland firms. Moscoso, a young, mainland-educated pharmacist, proved to be an energetic and effective salesman. As the head of Fomento (as it came to be known), Moscoso spread the word to mainland firms about the tax advantages of locating in Puerto Rico. With Moscoso's encouragement, the tax haven proved to be irresistible and by 1953, there were 291 new U.S. factories on the island.[58]

The first major firm to take advantage of the new tax situation in Puerto Rico was the textile manufacturer Textron. Shortly after the 1947 incentive was created, Textron closed six mainland mills, laying off roughly 3,500 employees, and began manufacturing in Puerto Rico. The Textron closure angered U.S. labor organizations, and under pressure from mainland legislators, Puerto Rico enacted the Industrial Tax Exemption Act of 1948. The 1948 law amended the 1947 law to prohibit tax exemptions to "runaway" firms whose relocation to the island caused mainland job losses.[59] The law left it up to the Puerto Rico economic development administrators, however, to determine which firms were "runaways" and, not surprisingly, they never found a single one. It would be 43 years before anyone seriously challenged Fomento on this issue.

Tax exemptions brought industry to the island. No other development strategy had been so effective so fast. The unprecedented investment that resulted from Operation Bootstrap established tax exemption as the heart of Puerto Rico's economic development strategy. Consequently, any subsequent challenge to this policy seriously threatened the stability of the island's economy and political situation. OCAW threatened the island's most important tax incentive and this explains the mobilization of Puerto Ricans against the union's Section 936 reform bid.

Origins of challenges to federal tax exemptions in Puerto Rico

OCAW's 1991-1993 attack on Section 936 was not the first time federal tax exemptions for Puerto Rico had been challenged and amended. The U.S. Congress made significant amendments to these laws in 1976, 1982, and 1986. In 1976, Congress recognized that federal tax exemption was a major factor in Puerto Rico's economic development but also saw that it had a high revenue cost relative to the number of jobs created and investments made by possessions corporations. To compel possessions corporations to invest more of their profits in Puerto Rico and to create more jobs, Congress replaced the Section 931 exemption with a credit (Section 936) against a firm's tax liability. It restricted the tax credit to income which was derived from the *active* conduct of business in the possessions. Income from passive investments, so-called "qualified possession source investment income" (QPSII) could only be exempt if it was reinvested in the possession.

The Tax Reform Act of 1976 also required the U.S. Department of the Treasury to publish annual reports on the operation and effect of the possessions system of taxation. The changes in 1976 originated in a broad effort by Congress to understand and quantify the budgetary impact of tax expenditures generally.[60] After 1976, it was the responsibility of the Treasury to track Section 936 and when it quantified the revenue cost of the tax law, Treasury became the primary advocate for reducing the tax benefit. Thus, Treasury's budgetary perspective shaped congressional views on the efficacy of Section 936 after 1976.[61] However, Section 936's impact on mainland employment did not become an issue for the Congress until OCAW's Whitehall campaign in 1991.

Congress again scrutinized Section 936 in 1982 after it became clear that U.S. parent corporations were abusing the tax break by allocating income from intangibles (usually patents, in the case of pharmaceuticals) to their Puerto Rico subsidiaries, even though the intangibles had been created by the parent company on the mainland.[62] This meant the parent would obtain deductions on the mainland (where taxes are higher and the deductions are more valuable) for the research and development expenses that gave rise to a patent and then claim the income from the patent as possession source income which would be exempt from taxation. In the Tax Equity and Fiscal Responsibility Act of 1982 (TEFRA), Congress closed this loophole by requiring Section 936 firms to prove they had a "significant business presence" on the island. TEFRA required firms to meet a 25% value-added test and show that 65% of the labor input derived from island production. It also raised the "active" trade requirement from 50% to 65% in a further attempt to close off the tax-sheltering opportunities available under the previous legislation.

In 1985, Section 936 came under attack again as a target for capturing revenues to reduce the federal budget deficit. The Reagan Administration threatened to eliminate Section 936 altogether but the Puerto Rico administration made a deal to save it by agreeing to actively support and promote the Caribbean Basin Initiative (CBI). The CBI, enacted in 1983 in the Caribbean Basin Economic Recovery Act (CBERA), was a Reagan administration plan introduced in the aftermath of the Grenada invasion to promote development in the Caribbean so as to thwart expansionist forays by Cuba. CBERA allowed duty-free importation of products "produced" in CBI countries.[63]

CBERA only required that 35% of an item's production value be manufactured in the CBI country to qualify for duty-free status. In the 1985 deal to save Section 936, Puerto Rico committed to spending $100 million of Section 936 funds annually on development projects in Caribbean Basin countries.[64] The Tax Reform Act of 1986 codified this twin-plant development plan and otherwise left Section 936 intact. The active business income requirement, however, was increased to 75%, again with the intention of encouraging greater employment and investment on the island by possessions corporations.

Origin and evolution of Puerto Rican industrial tax incentives

Beginning with the 1948 amendments to the Puerto Rico Industrial Incentives Act (PRIIA) of 1947, the Puerto Rican government adjusted its industrial tax incentives over the years also. Not surprisingly, the changes to the law reflected the changes in island politics and leadership. At the time of the law's inception, the island was governed by the Partido Popular Democratico (PPD), which became the party responsible for the establishment and ongoing advocacy of the island's Commonwealth status. During the years the PPD has held the governor's seat, they, for the most part, have expanded local tax incentives. Likewise, when the statehood party (Partido Nuevo Progresista or PNP) has been in power, insular tax exemptions have been reduced. The predominance of the PPD in island gubernatorial elections partly explains why exemptions have broadened more than they have contracted over the years.

In 1954, the Puerto Rico legislature amended the Industrial Incentives Act to allow possessions corporations to receive exemption for ten years after operations began. Previous versions of the incentive granted exemption for ten years from the time construction of the plant began. A 1963 amendment to the law granted complete exemption from taxation for longer periods if firms located their plants outside San Juan.

In 1976, Puerto Rico had a new governor, Carlos Romero Barceló, who advocated statehood and scorned the "rich industrialists who had thrived on the excessive tax exemptions."[65] As Congress replaced Section 931 with Section 936 and possessions subsidiaries were allowed to repatriate their profits tax-free to their mainland parents, Puerto Rico amended the Industrial Incentives Act to impose a "tollgate tax" on any dividends paid to the parent.[66] This tollgate tax amounted to the end of complete insular tax exemption for possessions corporations. However, a corporation could still reduce its tollgate tax liability by investing a portion of it in Puerto Rico development projects.

In 1978, the island government again amended PRIIA and this time, full tax exemption for newly locating companies was ended. The legislation created a declining schedule of exemption for property and income taxes. On the other hand, PRIIA 1978 extended the tax exemption to service industries. Banks, public relations firms, insurance companies, computer and communications service companies could now qualify for Section 936 status.

In 1984, the pro-statehood governor was defeated by the Commonwealth party leader, Raphael Hernandez Colon. The Hernandez Colon administration set about restoring the local tax exemptions that were reduced during the Romero Barceló administration. At this point in 1986, AHP was planning to expand its Ayerst-Wyeth Pharmaceuticals, Inc. (AWPI) in Guayama and build a new manufacturing facility that would employ 400 people at capacity.[67] AHP made it clear to the Puerto Rico government that the final decision to build the new facility was conditioned on the government improving the tax exemptions available under PRIIA 1978.[68] AHP even submitted proposed wording for the new legislation.[69] On January 24, 1987 Governor Hernandez Colon signed into law the new Puerto Rico Tax Incentives Act (PRTIA) at a groundbreaking ceremony on the AWPI site in Guayama. The new legislation mirrored AHP's proposals.

Specifically, the declining exemption schedule was eliminated and replaced by a flat 90% exemption. Firms could reduce their tax liability to 5% by investing up to half of their tollgate liability in Puerto Rico. The exemptions applied equally to service firms.

Notably, in spite of all the amendments to the Puerto Rico Industrial Incentives Act over the years, the prohibition against runaways remained intact. Of course, only a few people, on or off the island, knew it existed. Even Puerto Rico's Secretary of Labor admitted he was not aware of it.[70] As a result, no tax exemption grant was ever challenged until OCAW protested AHP's move to Puerto Rico in 1991.

OCAW's Second Legislative Drive

The first phase of OCAW's legislative effort ended with Hiler's election defeat in November 1990. Union leaders knew it would be a waste of time to pin their hopes on Hiler's successor due to his freshman status in the House. They needed a powerful Congressional advocate in order to continue their fight on Capitol Hill.

On the way back from their visit to Puerto Rico in December 1990, Leonard and Malloy flew to Washington D.C. to meet with the union's legislative director, Nolan Hancock, and various Congress members. Hancock arranged for the union leaders to meet with Arnold

Mayer whom Hancock believed could help the union in its Section 936 effort. Mayer, a retired former vice-president of the United Food and Commercial Workers Union, was a labor lobbyist who had helped bring the minimum wage to Puerto Rico in the early 1970's. Although, admittedly, he had "never heard of Section 936" prior to OCAW's involvement, he was game for the fight on the basis of the runaway issue. Mayer and Leonard coordinated the union's Congressional effort from that point on.

OCAW's first task was to find another sponsor for Section 936 reform legislation.[71] Hiler's departure from the House stalled the union's initial attempt, but it did open up the opportunity to enlist a legislator who would be more palatable to the AFL-CIO. In the spring of 1991, as OCAW's legal effort was getting underway, the union began to contact legislators in the House and Senate whom they thought would have an interest in their cause. They wanted a legislator who was sympathetic to labor, not afraid of intense lobbying by pharmaceutical and Puerto Rico interests, and had enough power to affect tax legislation. OCAW found its man in Representative Fortney "Pete" Stark, Democrat from California.

Stark was the fifth-ranking member of the House Committee on Ways and Means, the committee responsible for tax legislation. There were no major pharmaceutical plants or Puerto Rican communities in his district and Stark was very familiar with Section 936 and Puerto Rico politics. Stark was antagonistic toward both Section 936 and the island's pharmaceutical industry and generally was not counted among the friends of Puerto Rico.[72] In 1984, Stark led a Congressional investigation into a rum redistillation scheme run by the Romero Barceló administration. The investigation alleged that rum was shipped into Puerto Rico where it was redistilled and then sold as a Puerto Rican product. Stark sponsored legislation to outlaw the redistillation scheme and headed the congressional effort to prohibit Puerto Rico from sharing in future federal increases in liquor taxes, which cost the Puerto Rico government tens of millions of dollars beginning in 1984.[73]

Stark also sponsored legislation that would cost the pharmaceutical industry. An industry newsletter reported that Stark recently had introduced three pieces of legislation and was working on a fourth that could "prove harmful" to the pharmaceutical industry,[74] including a permanent revocation of the R&D tax credit and elimination of some tax deductions for advertising and promotional spending.

OCAW found it easy to convince Stark to take up its fight. In the spring of 1991, OCAW and Stark aides met to begin defining the constructs of their legislation. At this point, Congress and the nation were consumed with the Gulf War and its aftermath. In the glow of victory, hopes were high that the recession, which had begun only months before, would abate with the decline of oil prices to their pre-Gulf War levels. Congress was under no immediate political pressure to cut the deficit. The Treasury estimates of the cost to the budget of Section 936 had been published two years earlier and no Congressional action on the matter, save Hiler's, had been initiated. These political and economic realities plus the certain intense opposition of the pharmaceutical and Puerto Rican lobbies served to convince OCAW that there was not much point in attempting to cut back Section 936 benefits directly.

OCAW also knew that its most compelling argument so far was that mainland tax dollars were financing runaways to Puerto Rico under the auspices of Section 936. The runaway issue had to be the fundamental principle of their legislation not only because it was more likely to be endorsed by Congress members but also because it was a point that organized labor had tried to make for years. Runaways were the problem, not just Section 936. OCAW had to find a way to make its point legislatively that federal tax dollars should not be used to underwrite the shuffling around of factories from one U.S. site to another. They wanted to institute a mechanism which could identify a potential runaway and stop it before it located in Puerto Rico. So, as it had attempted to do 43 years earlier, organized labor initiated legislation which would deny Section 936 benefits to any new or expanding operation in Puerto Rico which had a "substantial adverse effect on employment at U.S. facilities." The difference was that, this time, Puerto Ricans would not make that determination, the "more dispassionate" U.S. Secretary of the Treasury would.[75] Stark introduced H.R. 2632 on June 12, 1991. Rep. Tim Roemer, Hiler's successor, was an original co-sponsor.

The Whitehall plant closed the following November. The union now hoped to influence the size of the severance payout either in an effects bargaining session or through a settlement of their lawsuits. As leverage, the RICO and WARN litigation held promise but these were long shots and AHP's considerable resources to both fight and stall these efforts was becoming more apparent as the discovery process progressed. Also, the NLRB hearings had not yet been held and though the Board eventually ruled in the union's favor, at this point in 1991 there was little to indicate that would be the outcome, especially since OCAW leaders viewed the Board as conservative. OCAW's legal actions were limited by the confines of the courtroom and the rules of civil litigation procedure. OCAW hoped that a parallel legislative effort would escalate the pressure on AHP. But the simple act of introducing a bill would not be enough, as the Hiler experience showed. As with their fight in the courts, OCAW's legislation had to have some weight behind it in order for it to endure opposition. Lawsuits require evidence and smart attorneys (and a friendly judge doesn't hurt either) in order to endure. Legislative initiatives require the support of powerful members of Congress.

Thus, in the months following the introduction of Stark's bill, OCAW solicited the support of other members of the House Ways and Means committee. By emphasizing the runaway issue as opposed to directly attacking Section 936, OCAW hoped it had a relatively pure bill which could be supported by organized labor's reliable allies. Also, Stark's bill did not suffer the apparent disadvantage of Republican sponsorship and thus garnered the support of the AFL-CIO. Other national unions joined with OCAW and encouraged Ways and Means committee members to support Stark's legislation. However, OCAW ran into significant opposition. Ironically, OCAW's main obstacle was the presence on the committee of Rep. Charles Rangel, D-N.Y., long one of labor's most solid supporters.

Rangel's district in New York City included East Harlem which is home to the largest population of Puerto Ricans outside of the island. Although Puerto Ricans in Puerto Rico cannot vote in Congressional elections, Puerto Ricans in New York City can. While OCAW had to work hard to make its legislation known on Capitol Hill, the union had only to hint at it to attract intense interest among Puerto Ricans.[76] Rangel was the fourth-ranking member on the Ways and Means committee and as such, enjoyed considerable influence especially among House liberals who counted on him to represent their interests in this powerful venue. Consequently, many of the legislators who may have been sympathetic to the union's cause did not demonstrate a willingness to oppose Rangel on an issue that would anger many of his constituents. OCAW decided it needed to build support for its initiative from the outside in.

With several federal legal actions underway and a bill in the House the union now had significant fodder for its public relations campaign. This foundation proved to be crucial not only because it kept the Whitehall workers' plight alive in a real sense but also because it served as a source of media angles by which OCAW could keep its story alive. OCAW's media campaign broadened its focus at the same time the Stark bill was introduced. The union released a list of 25 other plants it said had closed plants and transferred production from mainland facilities to Puerto Rico to take advantage of the Section 936 tax benefits.[77] OCAW wanted to show the scope of the impact of Section 936 and demonstrate it was a national problem that needed to be addressed by federal legislation. At the same time, the study localized the problem because it identified specific companies and cities that had been similarly affected. This helped union leaders as they tried to elicit support among legislators for their bill because they could point to Section 936 victims in the Congress members' own districts.

In the fall of 1991 when Whitehall closed, the U.S. presidential campaign was underway. Republicans were confident as President George Bush, who still enjoyed very high approval ratings for his Gulf War initiative, seemed unbeatable. The economy was in recession, however, and a groundswell of discontent was building. This recession differed from other economic downturns in that white-collar workers were losing their jobs as companies cut out layers of management and hired more temporary employees for professional positions. Also, as in the case of Whitehall in Elkhart, seemingly healthy, profitable operations were closing their doors and throwing out of work even highly trained blue- and white-collar employees. The business and financial press reported a "morale crisis"[78] as white-collar Americans worried whether their jobs would be the next to go.[79] The *Philadelphia Inquirer* ran a nine-part series entitled, *America: What Went Wrong?* which reported on situations, including the Whitehall closure, in which U.S. federal policies and tax laws seemed to benefit only the rich and to be responsible for the loss or exodus of American jobs. Section 936 fit easily into this category. The *Inquirer* series proved to be very popular and soon was compiled into a book of the same name that wound up on the *New York Times* bestseller list for 31 straight weeks. Also, the *Inquirer* gave away 400,000 free copies of its series before instructing the authors to get a publisher. Soon after, in the spring of 1991, Bill Moyers produced and aired a lengthy television documentary for PBS based on the Barlett and Steele book which spotlighted the Whitehall situation.

In early 1992, H. Ross Perot emerged as an independent presidential candidate and gave voice to millions of Americans who believed that the government itself was largely to blame for the nation's economic ills. Gerald Brown, former governor of California and a Democratic candidate for the presidency, echoed this sentiment and based his campaign on voter discontent with a governmental "system" that effectively locked out ordinary Americans and enabled "special interests" to make government policy for their own benefit. Candidate William Clinton shaped his campaign on voter worries over the economy and laid the blame for the country's problems on government policies that harmed middle-class Americans who "worked hard and played by the rules."

The U.S. Congress was not immune to these messages and in 1992, many pieces of legislation were introduced in both houses which sought to reorient the federal tax system to better serve the interests of American taxpayers. Section 936 reform was one of the tax laws targeted and thanks to OCAW, it came to exemplify what seemed wrong with the tax system generally. Altogether in 1992, the House of Representatives introduced five Section 936 reform bills and the Senate introduced one. Rep. Richard Schulze's (D-Pa.) legislation sought to repeal the tax break altogether. Byron Dorgan (D-N.Y.) and Les Aspin (D-Wi.) introduced bills in June that were similar to legislation introduced in the Senate by David Pryor (D-Ark.).[80]

Pryor was a long-time foe of Section 936 primarily because the tax law favored drug companies. He seemed not as interested in preventing runaway plants or saving mainland jobs as he was in attacking pharmaceutical industry interests. In the early 1980's he attempted unsuccessfully to repeal the tax break altogether.[81] In September 1991, as the Chairman of the Senate Committee on Aging, Pryor introduced legislation (S.2000) to deny Section 936 benefits to pharmaceutical companies who raised drug prices beyond a formula-based level. This legislation was said to be a counterattack to the industry's response to legislation he helped pass in 1990. The 1990 law required drug companies to sell drugs to the Medicaid program at the lowest price offered to other purchasers. "He accused the [pharmaceutical] industry of trying to subvert that law by raising prices for all."[82] OCAW had nothing to do with Pryor's interest in Section 936. In fact, Pryor appeared to distance himself from organized labor on this issue. Pryor's 1991 reform bid ultimately failed in March 1992 when he lost a battle on the Senate floor to attach his bill to a tax reform measure. Nonetheless, he would remain the Senate's most outspoken and widely quoted opponent of Section 936 until the tax incentive finally was cut back in August 1993.

Of all the Section 936 reform legislation introduced in 1992, the most important, and ominous for Section 936 supporters, was contained in a bill introduced by Rep. Daniel Rostenkowski (D-Ill.), chairman of the House Committee on Ways and Means. Called the Foreign Income Tax Rationalization and Simplification Act (FITRSA), this legislation was an attempt to answer the general frustration Americans had with government policies that seemed to work against them. It proposed to revise inequitable or counterproductive federal tax laws regarding foreign corporations and U.S. companies operating abroad that either made domestic firms unable to compete or provided incentives to move production out of the states. For example, one of the provisions addressed transfer pricing abuses which allowed foreign companies located in the U.S. to avoid U.S. federal income taxation. In this case the U.S. government effectively favored foreign firms over their U.S.-owned competitors. Another problem was the exodus of timber processing jobs that resulted from 1986 Tax Reform Act policies which favored raw log exports. Higher value-added timber processing jobs were lost to foreign raw log destinations. Rostenkowski's legislation reflected a general dissatisfaction among American voters with a federal tax system that appeared to work against the best interests of American workers and taxpayers. Rostenkowski's 180-page bill addressed dozens of tax provisions like these and Section 936 was one of them.

Rostenkowski's 1992 bill proposed to reduce Section 936 benefits by 15%. OCAW lobbied hard for the inclusion of an anti-runaway provision as the way to deal with Section 936 but was unable to attach Stark's runaway provision to the legislation. Instead, Rostenkowski proposed this modest 15% reduction of the tax incentive. Because of Rostenkowski's power as the chairman of the taxwriting committee, however, Puerto Rico supporters of Section 936 interpreted the move as a serious threat to the provision and reacted as if the legislation called for its repeal. They seemed to view it not as simply one more attack on Section 936, but rather as the culmination of the latest round of attacks on it. Also, the Puerto Rican press reported that OCAW had convinced other legislators, in the Senate as well as in the House, to scrutinize the tax provision for possible reform. The *San Juan Star* reported in October 1991 that Senator William Bradley, D-N.J., was ready to introduce a Stark-like bill in the Senate which would prohibit Section 936 tax benefits to runaways.[83] In March 1992, the *Star* reported that Rep. Andy Jacobs, Jr., D-Indiana was ready to introduce his own anti-runaway legislation.[84] Neither of these two bills ever was introduced but the presence of the many other reform bills, especially Rostenkowski's, fueled speculation and heightened fears that OCAW's attack on Section 936 was widening and ultimately would succeed to some degree. "While each of these measures poses only a marginal threat, the combination represents a more ominous force against Section 936, making the ground fertile for an eventual passage of some bill cutting back 936, not excluding one of the many now pending," reported a front page story in *Caribbean Business.*[85]

Nineteen hundred and ninety-two (1992) was a particularly inopportune year for Puerto Rican advocates of Section 936 and Commonwealth status to have to worry about an all-out attack on Section 936. It was an election year and OCAW's RICO suit against the top officials of the PPD (Hernandez Colón and Colorado) gave the PNP (the PPD's main opposition) ammunition because the suit characterized the PPD leaders as pawns of the 936 corporations. Also, although the U.S. Congress had derailed a 1991 initiative to authorize a plebiscite on Puerto Rico's political status with the United States, in 1992 the status plebiscite was still very much a priority for Puerto Rico political leaders.[86] The pro-Commonwealth PPD party held the Governor's seat then and PPD leaders viewed OCAW's attack on Section 936 as counterproductive to their goal of retaining Commonwealth status. The PPD's most persuasive argument against statehood had always been that Puerto Rico would lose the Section 936 incentive because the federal tax code would have to treat the island like every other state in the nation. OCAW's attack on Section 936 could be interpreted as proof that the island eventually would lose Section 936 benefits anyway. Thus, if OCAW's reform effort succeeded, Puerto Ricans might be more likely to vote for statehood. In short, OCAW's lawsuits and lobbying campaign posed serious threats to the goals of the PPD in 1992, and when Chairman Rostenkowski opened hearings on FITRSA in July of that year, the PPD and its supporters came out in force to defend Section 936.

The hearings lasted for two days and although over 50 witnesses testified about many controversial provisions of the bill, nearly all the discussion among the legislators focused on Section 936. Rep. Donald Pease, (D-Ohio) at one point admonished that the committee "ought not to overemphasize Section 936 as we tended to this morning—mostly because some of us are familiar with that and not so familiar with the other issues." Rostenkowski did not plan to send his bill to committee for mark-up in 1992 but OCAW's campaign represented an immediate threat and seemed to be gaining momentum. "We understand that we have to fight a short-term battle against each bill that comes up, as well as a long-term battle against misconceptions of 936 that have been spreading in Congress," explained Antonio Colorado, by then Puerto Rico's resident commissioner in Washington.[87] The defenders of 936 took the hearings seriously and, perhaps hoping for a preemptive strike, used this forum to make their case to legislators.

While Stark's influence on the Ways and Means Committee led to the inclusion of Section 936 in Rostenkowski's legislation, Rangel's relatively greater influence and opposition to the reform effort shaped the hearings and the tone of the committee's discussion. Witnesses who defended Section 936 far outnumbered the witnesses who opposed it. Of the 11 witnesses who testified about Section 936, only two, OCAW's Richard Leonard and Rep. Timothy Roemer from Indiana, spoke in opposition to it. The 936 defenders were numerous and represented a variety of interests and they all ardently argued the benefits of the tax break to Puerto Rico and foretold economic catastrophe if it were cut back. Rostenkowski's 1992 legislation proposed only a 15% reduction in Section 936 benefits and did not even mention runaways. By the testimony, however, one would have thought the bill called for a repeal of the legislation, so fervent was the defense of Section 936. Defenders of the tax provision included Antonio Colorado, who replaced Jaime Fuster as Resident Commissioner earlier that year, and the Puerto Rico USA Foundation (PRUSA) which represented mainland U.S. companies with operations in Puerto Rico. The Puerto Rico Manufacturers Association, Puerto Rico Chamber of Commerce, Puerto Rico Bankers Association, Banco Central Corporation, Government Development Bank for Puerto Rico, and the National Puerto Rican Coalition also testified for the tax break. Even the U.S. Department of the Treasury, long considered by many Puerto Ricans to be antagonistic toward Section 936, changed its position and advocated for no immediate change to the tax provision until they could study the options further.[88]

In spite of the impassioned testimony of pro-tax break witnesses, committee members continued to insist that Section 936 was indefensible because the revenue cost per job created was too high. Although the witnesses did counterbalance the union's portrayal of the tax break as simply corporate welfare, they offered little for legislators to take back to their own districts. Except in Congressional districts where there were many Puerto Ricans, Puerto Rico's economic problems simply were not as important to legislators as were their voting constituents' economic problems. Rep. Hiler learned the hard way that defending Puerto Rican interests did not win constituent support. Rep. Rangel said as much in the hearings, "don't you know that jobs in one's own district is more important to members than jobs in Puerto Rico?" he asked Luis Núñez of the National Puerto Rican Coalition. The mainland employment effects and cost to taxpayers were simply too compelling for legislators to ignore. It was clear by the end of the hearings that, one way or another, Section 936 was in jeopardy. Puerto Rico and the pharmaceutical companies located there stood to lose a great deal, in every sense of the word.

Congressional attention to reform Section 936 led to more political activity regarding the tax break's future. At the Democratic convention in New York City in mid-July, lobbyists on both sides of the issue worked to include a plank in the party platform which would spell out the Democrats' position on the tax incentive. Proponents of Section 936 were assisted by Mayor David Dinkins of New York who was co-chairman of the platform committee. Opponents' influence on the matter rested with Clinton campaign coordinators.[89] In the end, Section 936 proponents prevailed, but only in an eleventh-hour amendment to the official party platform. Puerto Rico PPD officials hailed the revision and said "it was the first time the Democratic Party back[ed] Section 936 openly."[90]

This assessment was an exaggeration since the platform never explicitly mentioned Section 936. Dinkins admitted, nevertheless, that the amendment was a response to the "sustained, all-out assault on Section 936" that had occurred in the months preceding the convention. The convention fight also was a precursor of the political battles over Section 936 that would materialize in 1993 after Clinton won the election.

JTPA Hearings

OCAW's battle on Capitol Hill included a direct attack on AHP in addition to the attack on the company's favorite Puerto Rican tax break. OCAW's RICO discovery turned up documents that seemed to suggest AHP fraudulently acquired federal dollars under the Job Training Partnership Act (JTPA) to train some of its workers in Guayama. OCAW claimed that AHP's receipt of a $500,000 on-the-job training grant (of which it used approximately $225,000) violated both the spirit and the letter of the JTPA. The union suggested AHP used the funds to assist in the relocation of Whitehall-Elkhart's production to Puerto Rico—a direct violation of section 141 of the act—and then only hired applicants it would have hired anyway. OCAW considered legal actions to address the alleged JTPA abuses. The union mentioned it in both RICO cases primarily to try to establish a pattern of racketeering and implied it was another example of how the Puerto Rico government used federal tax dollars to entice the relocation of mainland jobs. OCAW abandoned the idea of legal redress and decided it had more to gain by publicly embarrassing AHP over the matter. To this end, the union found a friend in Representative Tom Lantos, Democrat from California.

In February 1992, Greg LeRoy, the research director of the Midwest Center for Labor Research and a consultant to OCAW during the Whitehall campaign, contacted the professional staff person for Lantos on the House Employment and Housing Subcommittee for help in persuading the Department of Labor (DOL) to investigate possible JTPA abuses by AHP. OCAW had throughout the previous year attempted to convince the DOL of the need for such an investigation.[91] Amendments to JTPA to address widespread abuses of the law were pending in both houses of Congress and OCAW hoped to convince Lantos that hearings on AHP's use of JTPA funds would be an illustrative case in point.

Representative Lantos had made a name for himself among organized labor advocates for his practice of holding hearings on unethical and illegal corporate activities mostly regarding Occupational Health and Safety Act (OSHA) violations. Moreover, Lantos was well-known among OCAW campaign strategists. Arnold Mayer, OCAW's lobbyist during the Whitehall campaign was the vice-president of the United Food and Commercial Workers union when it became embroiled in a two-year battle with meatpacking giant, IBP (formerly Iowa Beef Processors). Lantos held hearings in that dispute over OSHA violations and ultimately threatened to bring criminal charges against top IBP corporate officers.[92] OCAW, too, had occasion in 1991 to appear before Lantos in a hearing on explosions at Phillips Petroleum refineries, again focusing on OSHA violations. OCAW encountered few obstacles in persuading Lantos to schedule hearings on AHP's use of JTPA training funds.

Lantos scheduled the hearings for July 30 and contacted AHP chairman and CEO John Stafford in a letter on July 7 to appear before the subcommittee to testify on AHP's use of JTPA training funds in Guayama, Puerto Rico.[93] The hearing was to examine AHP only; no other matter or companies were involved.

THE SETTLEMENT

July 1992 was the high-water mark of OCAW's Whitehall campaign against American Home Products. The union's political and adjudicative initiatives had become increasingly problematic for AHP and the Commonwealth defendants. OCAW led the opposition to Section 936 and now it was AHP who was held up as the tax-dodging corporate reprobate, even though there were dozens of other pharmaceutical companies who had been there longer and received far greater tax benefits. AHP took the hit for the entire industry and the only way to remove itself as the scapegoat of Section 936 opponents was to end put an end to the union's publicity campaign. Likewise, with the Puerto Rico gubernatorial election approaching, the Commonwealth defendants presumably wanted the negative publicity regarding them personally to end. They also wanted to remove the platform of the instigator of the latest attack on Section 936. The RICO suit and the circumstances of the shutdown were the foundation of the union's platform: eliminate the suit and the union would have nowhere to stand.

AHP indicated a willingness to settle the lawsuits as early as March 1992. At that point, Alan Kanner had recently signed on and a trial date for RICO I had been set for March 30. On March 6, the administrative law judge ruled in the union's favor on all seven remaining NLRB charges and ordered the company to engage in effects bargaining. AHP privately offered the union $10 million to drop the RICO suits altogether. By this time, however, OCAW had a contractual obligation with Kanner and decided AHP's offer was not enough to compensate both the workers and Kanner. Moreover, its legal initiatives seemed to be paying off; it had a trial date and a victory in the NLRB rulings. Flush with these successes, the union saw little reason to settle at that point in March.

WARN Suit Judgment

Shortly after the union turned down AHP's initial settlement offer, however, the momentum shifted. In April, OCAW suffered a formidable defeat. Both AHP and OCAW had asked Judge Miller for a summary judgment on the union's WARN allegations. On April 24, Miller granted the company's request and ruled in its favor. Miller explained that although AHP did violate the specificity requirements of the WARN Act, the company had acted in good faith by giving a blanket one-year notice of the plant's shutdown. "There simply was no secret in 1991 that the Elkhart Whitehall plant would close near the end of the year."[94]

The most detrimental aspect of the WARN judgment, however, was that the judge ruled that AHP had not made the decision to close the Whitehall-Elkhart facility until September 5, 1990, "when the chairman of the board approved the proposal."[95] The judge ruled that even though "timetables were developed; consolidation plans were discussed;...funds were appropriated ...and Whitehall had implemented a number of steps to occasion the shutdown," the final approval was not given until September 1990.[96] This ruling was a tremendous blow to the (by then) consolidated RICO cases. How could AHP have lied on its Guayama tax exemption application in 1986 regarding the effects on mainland jobs if it did not make the decision to close the Elkhart plant until 1990? The central issue in OCAW's RICO cases was *when* AHP decided to close the Whitehall plant. The WARN ruling threatened OCAW's RICO suits because it was now case law and as such could be used by AHP to convince Pieras to rule against the union on the grounds of "collateral estoppel." This, of course, is precisely what AHP did. On May 27, 1992, AHP and Commonwealth attorneys submitted a motion for summary judgment on the grounds of collateral estoppel. Judge Pieras set the motion aside.

Qualified Immunity Motion

On March 3, 1992, the Commonwealth defendants filed a motion for summary judgment based on, among other reasons, their assertion that OCAW's suit was really against the Puerto Rican government and thus they, as individuals, should be entitled to the protection of "qualified immunity." Pieras also set aside this motion without ruling on it for as long as he could. After the 1992 Puerto Rico gubernatorial election campaign was underway, Pieras' lack of action on the motion was at risk of appearing to be a political act. Federal judges in Puerto Rico are considered by some to be statehood advocates.[97] The Puerto Rico defendants in OCAW's RICO suit were members of the party favoring Commonwealth status (the PPD) and their opponents in the governor's race were members of the pro-statehood PNP. The judge could not hold off ruling on the qualified immunity motion too far into the election season without calling into question his judicial impartiality. The judge let it be known that he was likely to grant the defendants immunity. This presented a serious threat to the union's case because it would remove the Puerto Ricans as co-conspirators in the scheme to defraud. In other words, OCAW could not prove a conspiracy if the Puerto Rican individuals could not be held legally accountable as conspirators.

New "Proximate Cause" Case Law

A third problem arose for OCAW's RICO case by way of an "extremely significant" United States Supreme Court decision on March 24, 1992 regarding the "proximate cause" requirement of a RICO claim.[98] In this decision, the Court ruled that "there must be a direct relation between the injury asserted and the injurious conduct alleged." AHP filed a motion arguing that the OCAW workers were harmed only indirectly by the defendants' actions. The relevance of this ruling to OCAW's case was unambiguous and it cast a long shadow over the continued viability of the union's RICO suit.

Decision Bargaining Arbitration

One of the few bright spots for the union at this point was the arbitration hearing on the decision bargaining charge. OCAW found hope in a precedent-setting ruling in June 1991 by the NLRB in a case involving the Dubuque Packing Company. The Board ruled that this Iowa meatpacking company violated federal labor law by refusing to bargain with union workers over the decision to close one of its operations. In effect, the ruling placed the burden of proof on employers to show why they shouldn't have to bargain over a relocation.[99] OCAW expected the arbiter to rule in its favor sometime in the summer of 1992. The arbiter indicated to the union that he would order back payments from the time of the closure to the date of the ruling, amounting to almost nine months' pay.

Pressures Converge

Ironically just when their chances for prevailing in a trial seemed more promising than ever, AHP and the Commonwealth defendants decided to settle. Apparently, they had more to gain, or certainly, less to lose, by settling with the union. Thanks to OCAW, July presented the defendants with a series of highly disagreeable Congressional attacks that threatened both their reputations and their financial futures, not the least of which was the upcoming JTPA hearing. The House and Senate Section 936 reform legislation was gaining support and Fomento administrators were nervous that the ambiguity about the tax law would slow new investment in Puerto Rico. The publicity of a trial was sure to damage the PPD and undermine its party's reelection bid. Also, as compelling as the defendants' legal arguments were, a trial was risky because of the unpredictability of both Judge Pieras and of a jury. All these factors converged to compel settlement and on July 27, 1992, AHP agreed to pay the union $24 million to settle the RICO suits.

Conclusion

This was a remarkable settlement for a number of reasons. First, as Kanner pointed out, "no other worker in a state of the United States ha[d] ever recovered one cent from an alleged 'runaway' plant."[100] Secondly, this was the first time a union representing AHP workers had ever recovered anything more than contractually mandated severance from the company. The $24 million settlement was nearly two and a half times the company's original offer in March and over and above the six million dollar benefits package that was negotiated in the NLRB-mandated effects bargaining session earlier that spring. Most notable, however, is that from a national perspective, it was almost unheard of for any union anywhere in the United States to win anything in a plant closing battle. "In this day and age," Richard Leonard pointed out,"it's a resounding victory."[101]

The settlement was not without its critics, however. Some union members were irate that Kanner excluded local union participation entirely from the settlement discussions. None of the union leaders most involved with the campaign was present when the deal was made and union members in Elkhart were not given the opportunity to comment, let alone vote on the settlement offer.[102] Some claimed that the settlement was not even a quarter of the amount AHP received in tax breaks annually from Section 936.[103] Others questioned Kanner's $8 million fee in light of his late arrival to the case. Also, $24 million represented only about one year's payroll at the Whitehall plant in Elkhart.

The settlement ended the second phase of OCAW's legislative campaign. As part of the deal, OCAW agreed to end its campaign against the company but not its effort to reform Section 936. The union's third lobbying push began after the November 1992 election and ended a year later when the Congress passed the biggest cut in Section 936 benefits ever. Chapter Three examines this phase in the context of the union's media campaign.

NOTES

[1] Randall Samborn, "Plant Shutdowns," *National Law Journal* 13 , no. 47 (29 July 1991): p. 14.

[2] Credit for this point resides with Keith Knauss, Professor of Labor Studies at Indiana University, South Bend.

[3] Jim Miller, "Future murkier at Whitehall plant," *Elkhart Truth,* 27 April 1990.

[4] *American Jobs Stability Act of 1990,* 101st Cong., 2nd sess., H.R. 4831.

[5] U.S. Department of Labor, Bureau of Labor Statistics, *Occupational Compensation Survey, Elkhart-Goshen, Indiana Metropolitan Area,October 1991* (Washington D.C.: Bulletin 3060-62, August 1992). Also Keith Knauss, interview by author, November 1994.

6   Local business and political leaders organized a task force aimed at convincing AHP to continue operating in Elkhart. Initially, the union was not included on the task force. Malloy objected and subsequently the union was included. ("Task force aim: Keep Whitehall Laboratories here," *Elkhart Truth,* 5 May 1990.) Also, Editorial, "Whitehall jobs worth the fight," *Elkhart Truth,* 13 May 1990.

7   "Greed at Whitehall not from workers," (four letters to the editor), *Elkhart Truth,* 12 May 1990.

8   Connie Malloy, "Taking on American Home Products: A Description and Analysis of the Fight to Keep Whitehall Open" (Unpublished manuscript, Indiana University at South Bend, 1991), p. 8.22.

9   Connie Malloy, interview by author, 1 December 1994.

10   Jim Miller, David Schreiber, "Whitehall will close," *Elkhart Truth,* 1 October 1990.

11   Roemer was the son-in-law of Senator Bennett Johnston, D-La. who as chairman of the Senate Energy and Natural Resources Committee, was the most important member in Congress regarding Puerto Rico's political status. Johnston controlled the Pelican Political Action Committee to which the PMA and several influential Puerto Ricans contributed funds. According to the *San Juan* (Puerto Rico) *Star,* "a significant amount of the [Pelican] PAC's funds went to Roemer's campaign." (Harry Turner, "PDP link suggested to U.S. race," *San Juan Star,* 25 November 1990.)

12   NLRB case no. 25-CA-20931. Filed 11 November 1990.

13   Joseph Misbrenner, letter to Donald Boveri, 11 September 1990, (Malloy manuscript, "Taking on American Home," exhibit 6-2).

14   Ibid., chapter 6.

15   NLRB case nos. 25-CA-20972-1 and 25-CA-20972-2, filed on 31 October 1990.

16   NLRB case nos. 25-CA-20999-1, 25-CA-20999-2, and 25-CA-20999-3, filed 16 November 1990.

17   NLRB case nos. 25-CA-21032-1 and 25-CA-21032-2, filed 14 December 1990.

18   David Schreiber, "Union will ask judge to halt Whitehall move," *Elkhart Truth,* 4 January 1991.

19 The judge deferred the matter to arbitration under the *Collyer Insulated Wire* precedent. (*Collyer Insulated Wire,* 192 NLRB 837 (1967))

20 Malloy manuscript, p. 6.2.

21 Merrill Goozner, "Tax laws taking jobs, workers claim," *Chicago Tribune,* 27 September 1990.

22 Puerto Rico Tax Incentives Act of 1987, Section 8.b.1.

23 Question 28 of the tax exemption application as cited in *Oil, Chemical, and Atomic Workers International Union v. American Home Products, Corp.,* 92-1238.

24 Anne Mytych-DelPonte, "Puerto Rico tax breaks induce firm to relocate jobs, Indiana union says," *Employment & Training Reporter,* 21 November 1990, p. 234.

25 Ibid.

26 Ibid.

27 Harry Turner, "Tax break draws ire," *San Juan Star,* 18 October 1990.

28 Ibid.

29 "OCAW hits Puerto Rico move by AHP," *Chemical Marketing Reporter,* 239, no. 4, 28 January 1991.

30 1987 Puerto Rico Tax Incentive Act, Sect. 8(c)(2).

31 Harry Turner, "Congress may investigate 'runaway' plant," *San Juan Star,* 30 December 1990.

32 29 USC 1551(c).

33 *Oil, Chemical and Atomic Workers International Union v. American Home Products, Inc.,* 91-1093.

34 Ibid., (in "Memorandum of Law of Private Defendants in Support of Their Motion to Dismiss, p.2.)

35 Ibid., pp. 3-4.

36 Public Law 100-379.

37 Public Law 100-379, Section 8(a).

38 *Oil, Chemical, and Atomic Workers International Union v. American Home Products, Corp.,* S91-00050S.

39 Author telephone interview with Amy Beckett, attorney at Depres, Schwartz and Geoghahan representing OCAW, 19 February 1994. Also author telephone interview with Kary Moss at the Sugar Law Center in Detroit, Michigan, 10 February 1994.

40 Public Law 100-379, Section 5(b).

41 Jim Miller, "Whitehall hearing testimony shows split between sides," *Elkhart Truth,* 6 June 1991. Also, Jeff Kurowski, "Countercharges fly at Whitehall hearing," *South Bend Tribune,* 6 June 1991.

42 Robert Droecker and Richard Simon.

43 "Whitehall hearing testimony," *Elkhart Truth,* 6 June 1991.

44 Malloy manuscript, p.6.8.

45 *Oil, Chemical, and Atomic Workers International Union v. American Home Products, Corp.,* 91-1093. (Discovery ruling)

46 Ibid. (Reply of Private Defendants in Further Support of Their Motion to Dismiss, p. 15).

47 "Rebel with a cause, actually, several," *Business Week,* June 18, 1990, p. 157. and "Toxic world of Allan Kanner," *ABA Journal,* July 1989.

48 *Oil, Chemical, and Atomic Workers International Union v. American Home Products Corp.,* 92-1238.

49 Ibid., p. 15.

50 Ibid., p. 50.

51 Ibid., p. 32.

52 Ibid., p. 75.

53 Ibid., p. 36.

54 Harry Turner, "P.R. hit with $1 billion suit," *San Juan Star,* 26 February 1992.

55 James Dietz, *Economic History of Puerto Rico: Institutional Change and Capitalist Development* (Princeton, N.J.: Princeton University Press, 1986), p. 209.

56 Raymond Carr, *Puerto Rico: A Colonial Experiment* (New York: New York University Press, 1984), p.66.

57 For a variety of viewpoints and analyses of Puerto Rico's political structure and development programs during this period see, Dietz, chapters three and four, Carr, chapter two, and Edgardo Meléndez, *Puerto Rico's Statehood Movement* (Westport, Conn.: Greenwood Press, Inc., 1988), chapter four.

58 Dietz, *Economic History of Puerto Rico,* p.210.

59 Ibid.

60 See Chapter I endnotes 51 and 52.

61 Peter R. Merrill, "The Possessions Tax Credit and Puerto Rican Economic Development," in *Puerto Rico: Search for a National Policy* (Boulder, Colo.: Westview Press, Inc., 1985), p. 61.

62 Joint Committee on Taxation, *General Explanation of the Revenue Provisions of the Tax Equity and Fiscal Responsibility Act of 1982,* December 1982, pp. 81-83.

63 Specifically, CBERA "affords nonreciprocal preferential treatment to most products of designated Caribbean Basin countries by eliminating tariffs or, for a small group of products, by establishing tariff rates below the most-favored-nation (MFN) rate." (United States International Trade Commission (USITC), *Impact of the Caribbean Basin Economic Recovery Act on U.S. Industries and Consumers,* Eighth Report 1992 (Washington, D.C.: USITC Publication 2675, September 1993), p. vii.) CBERA countries include Antigua and Barbuda, Aruba, The Bahamas, Barbados, Belize, the British Virgin Islands, Costa Rica, Dominica, the Dominican Republic, El Salvador, Grenada, Guatemala, Guyana, Haiti, Honduras, Jamaica, Montserrat, Netherlands Antilles, Nicaragua, Panama, St. Kitts and Nevis, St. Lucia, St. Vincent and the Grenadines, and Trinidad and Tobago. The USITC issues annual reports on the operation of the CBERA program and analyzes some of the program's effects on U.S. industries and consumers.

64 James Dietz and Emilio Pantojas-García, "Puerto Rico's New Role in the Caribbean," in *Colonial Dilemma: Critical Perspectives on Contemporary Puerto Rico* (Boston: South End Press, 1993), pp. 109-112.

65 Carr, *Puerto Rico,* p. 15.

66 Dietz, *Economic History of Puerto Rico,* p. 301.

67 *OCAW-IU v. AHPC,* 92-1238. (p. 37, Stafford letter to Colon)

68 Ibid. (p. 33, AHP proposal to Colorado)

69 Ibid. (p. 35, AHP VP letter to Colorado)

70 Ibid. (p. 68)

71 The account of OCAW's legislative strategy is based partly on a series of conversations between the author and Arnold Mayer and Richard Leonard between February 1994 and January 1995.

72 "Rep. Stark's Sec. 936 bill to prevent plant "runaways" to Puerto Rico, *FDC Reports, Prescription and OTC Pharmaceuticals,* 53:24 (Chevy Chase, Md: FDC Reports, Inc., June 17, 1991).

73 Harry Turner, "Stark may spearhead House attack on 936," *San Juan Star,* 13 April 1991.

74 *FDC Reports,* June 17, 1991.

75 Harry Turner, "Anti-936 bill introduced," *San Juan Star*, 13 June 1991.

76 Ibid.

77 Midwest Center for Labor Research, "Jobs Exported to Puerto Rico," (Chicago, Ill.: Midwest Center for Labor Research) June 17, 1991.

78 Anne B. Fisher, "Morale crisis," *Fortune*, June 18, 1991.

79 "I'm worried about my job," *Business Week*, (cover story), October 7, 1991 and "Whose jobs will disappear next?" *Fortune*, October 7, 1991.

80 "Storm brewing over Section 936?" *Caribbean Business*, July 9, 1992.

81 Harry Turner, "Bill would link drug firms' 936 benefits to prices," *San Juan Star*, 25 September 1991.

82 Spencer Rich, "Report faults soaring prescription drug prices," *Washington Post*, 24 September 1991.

83 Harry Turner, "Sen. Bradley drafts bill to halt 'runaways,'" *San Juan Star*, 31 October 1991.

84 Harry Turner, "Indiana congressman joins battle against 936 benefits," *San Juan Star*, 23 March 1992.

85 "Storm brewing over Section 936?" *Caribbean Business*, July 9, 1992.

86 Martin Tolchin, "Senate panel derails bill on Puerto Rico referendum," *New York Times*, 28 February 1991, A,22:1.

87 "Storm brewing," p. 2.

88 Harry Turner, "Battle lines being drawn in coming review of 936," *San Juan Star*, 22 July 1992.

89 Jorge Luis Medina, "Support for 936 included in platform," *San Juan Star*, 16 July 1992.

90 Ibid.

91 U.S., Congress, House, Committee on Government Operations, Employment and Housing Subcommittee, *Waste and Misuse of Federal On-The-Job Training Funds*, 102nd Cong., 2d sess., 5 August 1992, p.82.

92 Charles Craypo, "Strike and Relocation in Meatpacking," in *Grand Designs: The Impact of Corporate Strategies on Workers, Unions, and Communities*, eds. Charles Craypo and Bruce Nissen (Ithaca, N.Y.: ILR Press, 1993), pp. 185-208.

[93] Employment and Housing Subcommittee, *Waste and Misuse,* p. 102.
[94] *OCAW-IU v. AHPC,* S91-00050S. (WARN summary judgment, p.26)
[95] Ibid. (p. 10)
[96] Ibid. (p. 11)
[97] Carr, *Puerto Rico,* p. 383.
[98] *OCAW-IU v. AHPC,* 91-1093 and 92-1238. (Plaintiffs' Memorandum in Support of Final Approval of the Proposed Settlement)
[99] "NLRB requires firms to bargain before relocating," *Wall Street Journal,* 17 June 1991.
[100] *OCAW-IU v. AHPC,* 91-1093 and 92-1238, (Plaintiffs' Memorandum of Support, p. 10)
[101] David Schrieber, "Whitehall settlement: A while before money comes, *Elkhart Truth,* 30 July 1992.
[102] Jeff Kurowski, "Some don't buy Whitehall deal," *South Bend Tribune,* 30, July 1992.
[103] Editorial, "Industry vulnerable on 936," *Elkhart Truth,* 31 July 1992.

III

Primetime, 60 Minutes and Michael Moore: The Media Campaign

> "The secret of the unidirectionality of the politics of media propaganda campaigns is the multiple filter system . . . the mass media will allow any stories that are hurtful to large interests to peter out quickly. . . . For stories that are *useful*, the process will get under way with a series of government leaks, press conferences, white papers or with one or more of the mass media starting the ball rolling. If the other major media like the story, they will follow it up with their own versions, and the matter quickly becomes newsworthy by familiarity."[1]

Since 1990, there is perhaps no "large interest" more politically mobilized and powerful than the disgruntled American taxpayer. The tax reforms of the 1980's, in which some Americans placed so much hope, left many disillusioned and with the sense that the federal tax system operates only to their detriment. Political party affiliation neither defined whether a person was disillusioned or her level of disillusionment, it simply differentiated the assignment of blame. Disgruntled taxpayers were Democrats, Republicans and Independents and they listened to and voted for whoever appealed to their belief that the system was seriously flawed. As candidacies lived or died on the issue of taxation, media organizations naturally assigned a great deal of importance to it. Moreover, as a target market group there seemed to be none broader or more numerous than that of the American taxpayer. Taxpayers became, in fact, a "special interest"; their willingness to use political and purchasing power endowed them with considerable influence and media organizations responded accordingly.

OCAW's resistance to the Whitehall closure and Section 936 reform effort attracted broad and sustained national press coverage. The media were willing to listen not because they were moved by the tragedy of the laid-off Whitehall workers, but because the union attacked the federal tax system. The workers, themselves, were not "worthy victims"; they were worthy only to the extent that they also were taxpayers. OCAW leaders smartly embraced this characterization as soon as they saw how persuasive it was. They consciously eschewed the fact that this was a union fight and instead highlighted the broader, more bourgeois tax equity issue. OCAW mainstreamed its message and this was the key to its success.

Some would argue with this point of view and attribute OCAW's success in attracting national press coverage to a liberal, anti-business bias in the U.S. mass media.[2] However, there were thousands of shutdowns in the 1980's bigger than Whitehall that received no national press coverage whatsoever. Organized labor tried for years to incite mainstream media coverage of the runaway issue with few successes. When the issue was covered, as in the case of the Mexican *maquiladoras*, it was portrayed as a labor issue rather than as a national problem created, in part, by taxpayer-financed tariff breaks. In terms of the number of U.S. manufacturing jobs lost, runaways to Mexico were a much more significant problem than runaways to Puerto Rico. Yet Congress was not compelled to act legislatively as it was in the case of Section 936. The difference was that OCAW defined Section 936 to the media as a problem for American taxpayers. Congress saw little political risk in ignoring runaways when the problem was defined as a labor issue. When taxpayers were identified as the victims, however, the legislators changed the law.

OCAW cleverly exploited the features of the mass media which tend to filter out coverage of issues important to organized labor.[3] This chapter examines how the union was able to engage and hold the interest of the media in its Whitehall campaign and Section 936 reform effort. It also demonstrates why this press coverage was so important to the outcome of these efforts. First, however and by way of historical perspective, it is necessary to explain the union's public relations activities in the context of contemporary union activism.

Corporate Campaigns: The Whitehall Battle in Context

Labor specialists and management consultants would characterize OCAW's battle to save Whitehall as a "corporate campaign." This appelation is variously applied to any substantial union initiative that employs "nontraditional tactics in an attempt to pressure [a] firm to change its behavior."[4] Unions most often initiate corporate campaigns to complement organizing drives, to compel firms to settle bargaining issues, or to avert a threatened plant closure. Labor advocates and adversaries alike view the corporate campaign as *the* emergent union response to objectionable corporate actions.

The basis for a corporate campaign is information. The union finds out all it can about the company and its managers then tries to use the information to find levers to pressure the company to accede to its wishes. The union examines the firm's financial relationships, stockholder priorities, regulatory history (including its record of compliance with safety, environmental, antitrust, utility, and tax laws) and use of federal and state funds. From this information, the union identifies the firm's vulnerabilities. It attempts to elicit support from groups who also could benefit from a change in the firm's behavior, whether or not the change the support group wants has anything to do with the immediate goals of the union. The union also employs sophisticated public relations techniques to elicit public support for its goals.[5]

In the case of the Whitehall shutdown, the lever was AHP's Section 936 tax benefit which was afforded by the opening of the Guayama plant. The support groups included Puerto Ricans opposed to Section 936, Congressional legislators and federal bureaucrats who wanted to reduce the budget deficit, labor organizations who wanted a solution to "runaways", and most important, disgruntled American taxpayers.

Corporate campaigns are a fairly recent phenomenon, dating back only to the late 1970's. During the 1980's, as permanent replacement workers rendered strikes nearly useless, unions turned increasingly to other strategies and actions which could affect the financial well-being of firms. Withholding work became not only less relevant but also much riskier for workers, and unions were forced to find alternatives. The corporate campaign has proved to be a viable and sometimes powerful alternative, and it essentially has replaced the strike as management's worst labor nightmare. Corporate campaigns now define what an activist union does.

OCAW's campaign to keep Whitehall open was indeed a corporate campaign, but from the standpoint of analysis, that label is almost beside the point. To examine OCAW's efforts only within the context of other corporate campaigns implies that there is a formula to them which when applied to another shutdown situation would work just as well. Also, the corporate campaign label precludes a full analysis of the events because it limits the discussion to those tactics which can be identified as typical corporate campaign techniques. As an example of the delimiting effect of the corporate campaign label, OCAW's own Section 936 lobbyist viewed his legislative reform efforts as separate from the "corporate campaign" the union was "running" against the company.[6] The threat to Section 936 was the essence of the pressure on AHP and as such was the foundation of the union's "corporate campaign." AHP did not settle the RICO suits out of concern that it would lose in court or because the negative publicity of the corporate campaign shamed them into it. These threats were simply not that compelling for a company the size of AHP. Thus, the contextual framework of the corporate campaign is important to understand from the standpoint of how OCAW's efforts fit into recent trends in labor union activities. As for explaining why they worked, however, this analytical perspective is less useful. It is no more informative than saying that a candidate for office won an election because he ran a political campaign.

Establishing Credibility and Accessing the Mass Media

Organized labor's biggest challenge in engaging the attention of the mainstream press is that it, at best, is viewed as just one more special interest whose fortunes and influence are in decline. At worst, unions are viewed as subversive to the interests of capitalism. Thus, when organized labor has a problem it wants aired publicly, it lacks credibility and legitimacy in the conventional popular press. In the Whitehall campaign, OCAW avoided these problems initially by enlisting the support of a conservative Republican Congressman. Although Malloy was not after Hiler's conservative credentials when she sought out his help, his sponsorship of the 1990 Section 936 reform bill legitimized OCAW's resistance to the Whitehall shutdown and had a palliative effect on the press' perception of it. Hiler's public support of the effort to save Whitehall purveyed at least three other advantages upon the union's media campaign. First, Hiler's unequivocally conservative credentials implied that this shutdown was not strictly a union problem. Second, his introduction of the bill in Congress was itself newsworthy, especially since he introduced it during an election year. Last and most important, the Hiler bill argued in favor of the interests of capitalism and the free market and thus eliminated the notion that the union's resistance to the shutdown was somehow a subversive act.

The local press covered the Whitehall situation for obvious reasons. Whitehall was a major employer in Elkhart and hundreds of residents stood to lose their jobs. Still, the union worked hard to ensure that the local media understood its goals and, in particular, its point that AHP's move out of Elkhart was motivated by the federal tax haven in Puerto Rico. The local media coverage attracted the attention of local politicians and compelled them to act on the workers' behalf. This active interest by elected officials added power and importance to the union's campaign which, in turn, led to broader media coverage and more political action.

There were hundreds of stories in the local press over the course of the campaign. The union used this coverage to communicate with Whitehall workers both during the campaign and after the settlement. OCAW made each article into a flyer and distributed all of them to workers at Whitehall-Elkhart and at AHP headquarters in New York. This proved critical to maintaining membership support throughout the many months of the campaign, especially after AHP severely limited Malloy's access to workers inside the plant in the fall of 1990.

Aware that local media exposure by itself would be unlikely to generate sufficient pressure on AHP to change its closure decision, the union worked hard to interest regional and national news organizations in its campaign. OCAW was assisted immeasurably in this regard by its association with Greg LeRoy and the Midwest Center for Labor Research (MCLR) in Chicago, IL. The MCLR, founded in 1982 by a former steelworker, is a labor advocacy organization with a history of dissension from mainstream labor leadership positions and policies. It bills itself as independent; labor insiders know this means it is independent of the AFL-CIO not that it is neutral on labor issues. At the urging of the Interfaith Economic Crisis Organizing Network, (a coalition of ecumenical organizations concerned about the effects of deindustrialization), the MCLR helped found the Federation for Industrial Retention and Renewal (FIRR) in 1988. FIRR is an association of 32 grassroots, activist labor organizations in 17 states in the U.S. whose stated purpose is to "save jobs and communities." As such, FIRR is a network of organizations and individuals motivated to assist unions prevent and resist plant shutdowns. A variety of FIRR affiliates assisted OCAW in various ways throughout the Whitehall campaign and after, when Section 936 reform was the union's priority.

During the ten or so years that LeRoy was the research director at the MCLR, he established personal and organizational credibility with a network of media contacts that was to prove invaluable for engaging the interest of the press in the Whitehall story. While his reputation and Rolodex of names and phone numbers did not ensure that the story would be picked up, they did facilitate the process at a point when time was of the essence.

As in any public relations campaign, publicity represented not the end but the means of OCAW's campaign. OCAW invoked the influence of publicity to create and escalate pressure on the people and institutions who could make a difference in whether or not the plant closed and to support its various legal actions and tax reform effort. Depending on the target and the reaction the union hoped to achieve, this pressure took one of two forms; it was either public or personal. Public pressure meant any action designed to attract public scrutiny of AHP's decisions and behavior. Personal pressure included actions designed to irritate and embarrass AHP managers and associates so they would act on the union's behalf simply to put an end to the irritation and embarrassment. This combination of personal and public pressure undertaken to support the union's legal and legislative initiatives proved remarkably effective, as the settlement and legislative gains demonstrate.

The following section outlines OCAW's media campaign activities from the fall of 1990 when the international union joined the Whitehall fight until July 1992, when AHP settled the RICO lawsuits. It characterizes them as either public or personal pressure tactics and also identifies the object of each pressure tactic and the goal the union hoped to achieve by it.

PUBLIC PRESSURE

Social Cost Analysis

LeRoy joined the Whitehall campaign in a limited way shortly after Richard Leonard and the OCAW-IU became involved in July of 1990. LeRoy did not initially handle the union's media effort. OCAW hired a New York-based public relations firm with the hope that it would be able to access large media markets. LeRoy's first project on behalf of the campaign was a "social cost analysis" of the impact of the Whitehall closing on the Elkhart economy.[7] This survey-based study examined Whitehall's local supplier relationships and the buying patterns of Whitehall workers to estimate the effect on both if the plant closed and workers suddenly lost their income. The MCLR used a U.S. Department of Commerce input-output model to attempt to quantify the "ripple effects" of a Whitehall shutdown.[8] The MCLR had undertaken similar analyses in other plant closing situations and thus was able to prepare the report in a matter of weeks. OCAW introduced the report at a press conference in September with Rep. John Hiler and other local government officials.[9]

The report and press conference were important not only because they attracted media attention but also because they reinforced the idea that a Whitehall shutdown was not an insular union problem. OCAW hoped to broaden its support base by quantifying the likely effects on the community as a whole. By showing how much the shutdown would cost the Elkhart economy, the union sought to compel greater action by local officials to save the plant. An earlier MCLR social cost analysis of a threatened plant shutdown by Trico Products Corp. in Buffalo, New York had done just that. The costs detailed in the Trico social cost analysis helped to convince New York state officials to fund a joint effort by union leaders and management to modernize and streamline Trico's Buffalo operation. As a result, Trico kept the plant open and 1,400 workers were laid off instead of 2,500.[10] This was the sort of outcome OCAW wanted to achieve.

As sure as OCAW leaders were that AHP already had made the decision to close Elkhart, they found implicit hope in the fact that the company had not yet announced it officially. Throughout the summer of 1990, AHP said it was conducting a study of its operations worldwide and insisted it had made no decisions regarding the Whitehall plant in Elkhart. Rep. Hiler and Mayor James Perron of Elkhart met with AHP managers in New York earlier that spring to try to clarify the firm's plans and convince company officials of the benefits of operating in Elkhart. AHP continued to insist the closure decision was only under consideration.[11] OCAW hoped that MCLR's detailed picture of the social and economic costs of a Whitehall closure would compel other government officials to look for ways to compel AHP to stay.

Labor Day 1990 Parade

Three days prior to the MCLR report, OCAW sought to publicize the Whitehall situation to local and state elected officials and candidates for office at Elkhart's Labor Day Parade.[12] Hundreds of union members turned out for the parade. OCAW hoped to compel action by the state and local politicians to investigate ways to save the plant. Malloy had contacted and visited with state and local legislators prior to the parade but the broad show of support among union members and other parade participants added political weight to the event and to the union's shutdown fight. The union's subsequent MCLR report lent substance to its parade day call for action. Also, the parade participation was an effective and efficient use of union resources to the extent that it reminded dozens of politicians of the plight of the Whitehall voters all in one afternoon.

Whitehall and Me: Michael Moore Visits Elkhart

AHP officially announced on October 1, 1990 that it would close Whitehall thirteen months later. The announcement galvanized the union and intensified its commitment to fight. As in many situations in which a shutdown is only threatened, some Whitehall workers feared prior to the official announcement that fighting back would give the company a reason to close the plant. Thus, they resisted categorical recrimination of the company and urged union leaders to hold back their sharpest criticisms. Union actions to this point focused on U.S. tax law inequity and worker solidarity. Once AHP announced the shutdown, however, OCAW saw no reason to temper its denunciations. With little left to lose, OCAW abandoned its defensive posture and began in earnest to seek public relations opportunities that would force the company to reexamine its shutdown decision. [13]

In October, Malloy wrote to Michael Moore to ask for his support in the shutdown effort. Moore was a filmmaker of some acclaim, especially among unionists and CEO's, for his sardonic, quasi-documentary film, *Roger and Me*. The film details Moore's unsuccessful attempts to obtain an audience with Roger Smith, then Chairman of the Board of General Motors Corporation, to discuss the effects of GM plant shutdowns on Flint, Michigan and its residents. The film portrayed GM executives as oblivious and unconcerned and juxtaposed their lavish work- and lifestyles with the destitute lives of unemployed, former GM workers. The film was a critical and popular success and it humiliated its corporate targets. OCAW hoped Moore's involvement in the Whitehall shutdown would achieve the same effect. OCAW also saw public relations value in Moore's support.

OCAW invited Moore to a press conference in Elkhart and suggested a *Roger and Me*-type, on-camera interview attempt at AHP's corporate headquarters in New York. "Touched" by Malloy's letter and description of the workers' plight, and cognizant, perhaps, of the comedic potential of a visit to the maker of Preparation H (a hemmorhoid medication), Moore agreed to help OCAW. Within two weeks, Moore was in Elkhart with a film crew. [14]

Moore's visit was picked up by the wire services but attracted mostly regional press coverage. [15] One major international publication, *The Economist*, however, reported on Moore's visit and the union's fight to keep the plant open. [16] Moore, who paid his own way to Elkhart, agreed to let the union use footage of his visit for a documentary. Although he never went to AHP's headquarters in New York, the union left the impression that it was only a matter of time before film footage of the Whitehall situation ended up in another Moore film.

Within a week of Moore's visit, AHP doubled the number of layoffs it earlier had announced for the fourth quarter of that year. OCAW said the action was retaliation for Moore's visit and filed a NLRB charge against the company. The company said the layoffs corresponded to declining production requirements. The Board eventually ruled in favor of the union.

Attacks on AHP's Corporate Image

OCAW undertook a number of actions which were designed to impugn the corporate reputation and image of American Home Products and bring questionable activities to the attention of consumers of AHP products and to stockholders and financial analysts. This was archetypal corporate campaign politics; try to disrupt AHP's economic relationships and thus bring market forces to bear on its behavior. Although, this type of action has taken many forms since it first was used in 1976 by Ray Rogers and the Amalgamated Clothing and Textile Workers Union (ACTWU) against J.P. Stevens, it is not unlike a boycott in its effect on a firm. Because of the variety of approaches, it defies a simple label such as "boycott" affords. It is a much more comprehensive version and requires a more sophisticated and detailed understanding of the firm's financial vulnerabilities.

OCAW used this tactic very successfully in an earlier campaign involving the German chemical manufacturer, BASF. In that campaign, OCAW spotlighted the company's environmental record and helped foment broad public opposition to BASF expansion plans. Although, OCAW's entire campaign against AHP could be characterized as an attack on the company's reputation and corporate image, the discussion in this section focuses on those activities which directly or specifically denounced the company for behavior unbecoming its public persona as a manufacturer of health care products.

OCAW's biggest obstacle in this regard was that "American Home Products" was not a familiar name to most consumers. AHP did not include its corporate name in any of its advertising or on any of its labels. Instead, it stressed brand names and barely identified even the subsidiary company that manufactured the products. Thus, although most Americans probably would recognize AHP's products, Advil, Anacin and Dristan for example, few would recognize them as products of AHP. This would be a problem for campaigns against any pharmaceutical company since advertisements for drugs, especially over-the-counter products, promote brand names rather than corporate identities. This was an even bigger problem for OCAW because of the nearly complete absence of association between AHP and its brand name products. OCAW could not attack AHP's reputation among consumers because the company had none. Thus, OCAW's options for public castigation of AHP's image were limited to those arenas in which AHP had an identity. It focused, therefore, on physicians, AHP stockholders, and AHP employees.

Physicians. In October, just after they received the plant closing announcement, local unionists traveled to AHP's New York City headquarters to picket and protest the Whitehall closing. The union scheduled its demonstration to coincide with the American Public Health Association's annual meeting. OCAW circulated a petition at the meeting which called into question the Whitehall closing and stated it "may cause the medical community to re-evaluate the trust and confidence that [it] placed in [AHP's] products." OCAW gathered hundreds of signatures from the meeting and passed out copies of the petition to employees, including company officers, as they arrived for work at AHP headquarters in midtown Manhattan. OCAW members were accompanied by a group of approximately 50 doctors and other health care professionals in lab coats as they passed out the petitions. OCAW said they also had pledges from some of the doctors at the rally to "voice their displeasure with AHP when salespeople from the corporation's companies call[ed] on them in their offices."[17]

Several national news organizations showed interest in the demonstration, including CBS News, National Public Radio (NPR), and NBC. *Marketplace*, a daily business news program on NPR, included a story about the Whitehall situation on the day of the protest.[18] NPR aired a segment as well.[19]

AHP Stockholders. OCAW attempted to make AHP stockholders aware of the Whitehall situation with a number of "shareholder actions." In April 1991, union members and leaders demonstrated and spoke during a question-and-answer session at the company's annual meeting. Their attendance at this meeting had no discernible influence on the corporation's position on this matter nor did it result in any influential media coverage. It did, however, provide union members with the opportunity to confront AHP chairman and CEO John Stafford face-to-face and irritate him and other corporation officers.

The U.S. federal government requires all publicly traded

companies to hold annual stockholder meetings and to give formal notice of the meetings to all stockholders of record. Stockholders or their proxies are entitled to attend annual meetings and to vote on all matters that require stockholder approval. Unions (and many other activist reform organizations) use the occasion of the annual meeting to raise questions and engender support among other stockholders to try to prompt corporate behavioral changes.[20]

Shareholder actions vary in terms of their intent and efficacy and shareholders must work within the confines of the meeting framework established by the company and the Securities and Exchange Commission (SEC). This framework and set of procedural rules can limit the options of an organization that wishes to challenge a company's action at an annual meeting, especially if the issue in question requires an urgent hearing. To initiate a stockholder resolution, for example, the SEC requires the stockholder to have held at least $1,000 of stock for at least one year prior to the filing deadline. The filing deadline is often five or six months before the annual meeting, putting the advance holding requirement at around 18 months. In a plant closing situation this lead time can be prohibitive. OCAW initiated a shareholder resolution but because of the lead time required, it could not be submitted until after the plant closed, at the 1992 annual meeting.

Because the plant already was closed, the resolution sought to establish a "Facilities Closure and Relocation of Work Committee."[21] This committee would be comprised of board members and employee representatives and would advise the company as to the impact of plant closures or work relocations on communities in which plants and work are located. The union expected the company to "chafe at the implication that responsibility over plant closing decisions be shared with worker representatives."[22] Moreover, union-related proxy resolutions are not very successful anyway. One study showed that the average levels of support for union proxy resolutions lag behind the average levels for all public interest proxy resolutions.[23] Indeed union proxy resolutions that deal with social justice issues do well if they receive five percent support from stockholders.[24]

Nevertheless, despite the slim chances for the resolution, OCAW proceeded with it to widen the publicity of the union's fight and to confront top AHP officials with the human consequences of the

Whitehall shutdown. Shareholder resolutions are mailed to every stockholder with the company's notice of its annual meeting and proxy statement. Each stockholder is asked to vote on the resolutions. Only three percent of those voting supported OCAW's resolution.[25]

Proxy resolutions have been used somewhat more successfully by unions in other campaigns, but to engender broader stockholder support requires a concentrated and expensive effort.[26] At the April 1992 stockholder meeting, OCAW's members at Whitehall already were terminated and OCAW had no remaining members at any other AHP facility. OCAW chose instead to expend its limited resources on the legal and legislative initiatives that, at the time of the 1992 annual meeting in April, were showing considerable promise.

AHP Employees. OCAW sought to enfold as many AHP employees into its battle with the company as it could in order to broaden its base of support. For example, at the company's corporate headquarters, the union wanted to make employees aware of the shutdown situation to demonstrate the human consequences of their bosses' business decisions. Beginning shortly before AHP's official shutdown announcement, Stanley Fischer, a former OCAW local union president from New Jersey who led an earlier OCAW fight to avert a 3M plant closure in Freehold, New Jersey, began regular leafletting in front of AHP headquarters in New York. Fischer distributed copies of press accounts over a period of five months that detailed the union's actions and the issues involved. The union hoped this awareness would engender suspicion and hostility among employees towards top managers and ultimately foment dissent. In fact, the handbills openly solicited supporters and information from headquarters employees. This penetration into the corporate offices was meant to serve as additional pressure on the corporation's decisionmakers. The union hoped to annoy AHP managers and poke at their consciences to the point that they would consider ways (i.e., keep Whitehall open or settle with the union) to make the matter go away. Short of that, OCAW hoped their provocations would cause AHP to make mistakes simply out of anger and exasperation.

Access to employees entering AHP headquarters, including top managers, was easy due to the location of the building on Third Avenue in New York City. There was only one way in from the street which virtually assured distribution opportunities.[27] Fischer's (and later, his associates') presence was an incessant reminder of the Whitehall plant and the workers who would soon lose their jobs. Before managers could get through the front door, they were confronted with the sorry plight of the workers in Elkhart. OCAW hoped that no matter how sure they were that the decision to close Whitehall was the right one, AHP managers probably would not enjoy facing the issue the first thing in the morning.

Fischer's presence at the headquarters came to an end in March 1991. Fischer was about to begin a new job with the state of New Jersey's Division of Consumer Affairs when AHP sued him for misrepresenting himself at a Pharmaceutical Manufacturers Association (PMA) meeting. In February, Fischer had arrived at the PMA offices in Washington, D.C. and identified himself as being "from Whitehall." As a result, he gained access to the "non-public" meeting, received printed materials and was privy to other information intended only for AHP and other PMA members. Fischer and OCAW argued he had never sought to hide his identity (he gave the receptionist his name) and claimed AHP officials were well aware of Fischer's association with OCAW and the Whitehall closing campaign. Of course, AHP officials who could identify him and his association with OCAW were not sitting at the receptionist's table nor were they at the meeting. The court enjoined Fischer from misrepresenting himself further and from distributing or discussing any materials or information he obtained at the meeting. OCAW's defense of Fischer cost the union nearly $75,000 in legal fees.

Fischer's departure did not end the leafletting in front of the company's headquarters. Two associates of Fischer continued headquarters distributions through mid-1992. To augment the direct distributions to AHP headquarters employees, the union routinely mailed press accounts of the situation to a list of AHP managers. OCAW also targeted AHP salespeople, board members, major stockholders, and pharmaceutical trade association members for its mailings, to inform them of the corporation's and the union's actions. OCAW assembled dozens of press accounts about the Whitehall situation and other unrelated, but objectionable AHP policies and produced its own version of an "Annual Report." The union distributed these at both the 1991 and 1992 stockholder meetings and sent them to its various campaign mailing lists.

Besides headquarters employees, OCAW hoped to inspire the support of employees at other AHP plants whose production levels or lines may have been affected by the opening of the Ayerst-Wyeth plant in Guayama. Two AHP stateside subsidiaries participated in the manufacturing of Advil in addition to British contract manfacturer, Boots, Ltd.; one in Rouses Point, New York and one in Hammonton, New Jersey. Because Advil production comprised most of the Guayama manufacturing activity at that time, OCAW insisted Rouses Point and Hammonton suffered lost production and jobs to Guayama. Although Boots, Ltd. manufactured most Advil products (Hammonton only packaged Advil), laid-off workers from these facilities ultimately were included in the RICO II class action suit against AHP. AHP denied these plants lost work to Puerto Rico and pointed to an increase in processing of Advil at both facilities. OCAW leaders, during discovery ordered under its consolidated RICO suits, visited the Hammonton, Rouses Point, and Guayama facilities and said they found evidence that showed AHP rerouted production machinery from Guayama back to Hammonton after OCAW initiated its campaign.[28]

Thanks to the access to AHP internal documents the RICO discovery orders afforded OCAW leaders, they believed that the Guayama facility had and would continue to affect the production levels and lines at Rouses Point and Hammonton. They had a much more difficult time convincing the employees at those plants, however, and faced opposition and fear each time they attempted to foster support. In July 1991, before the Whitehall-Elkhart plant closed, OCAW caravanned to New York for a demonstration at AHP headquarters. Members took this opportunity to visit the nearby Whitehall Hammonton facility in south central New Jersey and distribute handbills explaining the Whitehall-Elkhart closing and its connection to the operation in Guayama. The flyers also asked for the support of the Hammonton workers and warned them they could be next. Although they backed up traffic while lining up to receive the flyers and ask questions about the Elkhart shutdown, most Hammonton workers resisted OCAW's solicitations for support.[29] Less than three years later, AHP announced it would close the Hammonton facility within 20 months. Nine hundred workers would lose their jobs.[30]

OCAW's attempt to solicit support from workers at the Rouses Point plant was met with a chilly reception by workers there. Ironically, Rouses Point production employees were unionized (Hammonton was not) and represented by the International Chemical Workers Union (ICWU). OCAW believed local and national ICWU leaders resented OCAW's campaign against AHP because the Rouses Point Ayerst production facility gained new production lines during this period. In fact, in 1992 there were more total employees and more employees involved in production at Rouses Point than at any prior time.[31] Also, ICWU leaders respected Joseph Bock, AHP's senior executive vice-president of industrial relations, and viewed AHP's labor relations policies as beyond reproach. They distanced themselves from OCAW's campaign presumably because it reflected badly on Bock and the company.

Specialty Trade Publications

Early on in the campaign, OCAW targeted specialty trade publications to publicize the Whitehall plant closing issues. This proved to be one of the most efficacious media tactics the union tried. The complexity of the issues provided a number of key media angles. Database and library searches turned up scores of relatively obscure but relevant trade publications which LeRoy seized upon as publicity opportunities. By the middle of the campaign, LeRoy was faxing press releases to about 95 media outlets.[32] In press releases to these publications, LeRoy took great pains to be as "fact-filled" and relevant to each publication's readership as possible, often playing down the fact that this was a union-led dispute. The approach worked and he placed stories with pharmaceutical and other health industry trade publications, law journals and newsletters, Puerto Rican and Caribbean news outlets, and alternative or "progressive" periodicals. As stories were published, LeRoy used them as background material for subsequent media solicitations. Each published piece lent credence to the newsworthiness of the situation. LeRoy used the volume and variety of the coverage to speak for the importance of the union's efforts and the story soon became "newsworthy by familiarity."

The best example of this phenomenon was the publication in *Corporate Finance* of an article highly critical of AHP's handling of the Whitehall campaign.[33] The article outlined in detail the closure and blamed it on Section 936 tax breaks. It also accused AHP of bumbling its response to the union's campaign saying, "the company's left-footed PR played right into critics' hands...even financial exectives sympathetic to American Home's motives may view the Elkhart closing as a blunder that will force them all to spill confidential information." The magazine was a business publication whose heavyweight title belied its fledgling status. Thus in the original publication, the article probably did not reach a very wide or influential audience. OCAW made sure AHP saw it, however, and the company responded in a letter to the editor sharply criticizing the publication for its one-sided coverage.[34] By then, the union had adopted the article as its favorite public relations tool. The union found it immensely useful that even a "well-respected business publication such as *Corporate Finance"* decided that AHP had "obviously deviated from responsible and ethical behavior in its business dealings."[35] OCAW used the article to legitimize its struggle to other potential media organizations. Moreover, as it lobbied for support of its legislative agenda in Congress, OCAW discovered that the article was highly effective for engaging the attention of legislators skeptical of the union's motives.[36]

The Puerto Rico and Caribbean Press

While articles in "respectable" publications like *Corporate Finance* helped create the impression that OCAW's campaign was mainstream and worthy of a closer look, the most influential press coverage in terms of creating real political pressure was the coverage by the Puerto Rico and Caribbean press. The story of OCAW's attack on Section 936 was itself relevant and newsworthy to these media organizations and it certainly would have been covered with or without OCAW's salesmanship. However, the union's seemingly incessant newsworthy actions, like the Stark bill and list of 25 other "runaways", and each action's accompanying publicity effort combined to build the impression that the recent Section 936 effort resulted from a broad-based groundswell of mainland animus toward the tax incentive. "Indiana plant's move to P.R. becomes national issue," announced a headline in the *San Juan Star* early in the campaign.[37] Both the volume and urgent tone of articles in the local press helped pressure Puerto Rico government officials and island business leaders to look for ways to end OCAW's campaign.

In the period 1991 through mid-1992, OCAW publicized the RICO suit and its alleged La Fortaleza[38] political shenanigans, to motivate Hernández Colón administration officials to pressure AHP for a settlement. OCAW portrayed Hernández Colón and his administration as pawns of the Section 936 industry both in the RICO complaints and in the local press. At a press conference to announce RICO I, union leaders denounced island administration officials for illegal acts of "omission and negligence" that "lent support to this law-breaking activity."[39] In RICO II, OCAW described "schemes" and "deals" between the company and the Commonwealth officials and pointed out three apparently unreported campaign contributions from AHP to Hernández Colón's reelection committee during October 1988.[40] A letter from AHP CEO John Stafford to Hernández Colón informing him of a campaign contribution was released to the Puerto Rico press. There appeared to be no official record of the amount of the contributions or whether the contributions were reported as required under Puerto Rico electoral law. Stafford did make a personal contribution of $500 but was under no obligation by Puerto Rico to report it. Nevertheless, OCAW played up the ambiguities about the contributions to the press and subsequent news accounts were full of suspicion and innuendo."Who did Stafford send the contribution to and for how much?" asked one Puerto Rico news report.[41]

OCAW's publicity about the relationship between the Commonwealth officials and AHP officers presaged an intense and relentless publicity campaign if the RICO case were to go to trial. This was the last thing the PPD needed just months before the gubernatorial election and while Congress debated the future of Section 936. In response, the Puerto Rico administration attempted to quell the union's runaway concerns by offering to enact local legislation which would prevent runaway plants from relocating to Puerto Rico.[42] OCAW rejected the proposed regulations in February 1992 on the advice of Puerto Rico attorney and statehood advocate Luis Costas Elena, who said that the proposed regulations lacked a provision for judicial review of administrative appeals decisions. In other words, critics of a firm's move to the island would have no opportunity for an independent review of the firm's request for tax exemption. Costas Elena also claimed the regulations could be altered without notice.

After the union rejected the proposals for stronger island regulations against runaways, the Commonwealth officials sought to extricate themselves entirely from the RICO suits and attendant negative publicity. On March 3, 1992, the Commonwealth defendants filed a motion for summary judgment based on their claim as government defendants for "qualified immunity." Pieras reset the RICO trial date for August 3 and weeks passed with no official word from him on the matter. It became apparent that even if Pieras were to grant the Commonwealth defendants immunity, it would not happen prior to the trial and it would not put an end to the publicity. Arguably, the union would have the right to appeal the judgment immediately since such a ruling would effectively nullify the union's RICO conspiracy argument.[43] The appeal process would create more negative publicity opportunities, and with the election at hand, this had the potential to undermine the PPD reelection bid. Thus, the threat of trial publicity was real and persuasive.

Their status as elected officials naturally made the Commonwealth defendants more publicity-sensitive than AHP. However, AHP's future in Puerto Rico depended on the continuation of Commonwealth status on the island, so AHP had to be concerned when OCAW's publicity threatened political advocates of continued Commonwealth status, namely, the PPD. Political parties in Puerto Rico, for the most part, differentiate themselves by their position on the island's political status with regard to the United States. Thus, a political defeat of the Commonwealth party (PPD) has always meant a victory for statehood advocates. (Advocates for an independent Puerto Rico represent only about four percent of the voting population.[44]) The statehood party (PNP) candidate in 1992, Pedro Rosselló, promised to push the U.S. Congress for a status plebiscite.[45] A Rosselló victory would implicitly indicate that there was an electoral preference for statehood on the island and statehood would mean the end of Section 936. More to the point, it was not at all clear whether a PNP governor and resident commissioner could be counted on to defend Section 936 as vigorously as did their PPD counterparts. Therefore, as a Section 936 beneficiary, AHP was not immune to the publicity pressures on the Commonwealth officials in 1991 and 1992.

Pharmaceutical Industry

Nor was the company immune to pressures from other Section 936 companies on the island, especially from pharmaceutical companies who had the most to lose by a change in either Section 936 or the island's status. LeRoy placed articles in industry periodicals and newsletters throughout the campaign to spread the word about OCAW's court challenge of AHP's move to Guayama and legislative challenge to Section 936. The union as early as January 1991 suggested it intended to widen the scope of its investigation into Section 936 abuses. "OCAW has evidence 'that suggests a similar pattern of job transfers at Johnson & Johnson, Merck, Warner-Lambert, Bristol-Myers Squibb, Anaquest/BOC and Teledyne Turner Tube...[the union] cautioned that the suit against American Home Products 'may not be the last of its kind.'"[46] OCAW's June 1991 list of 25 other "runaways" was a bellwether that the union meant to make good on its threat.

By spreading the word to AHP's competitors, OCAW hoped to isolate the company from its peer group and get others to pressure AHP to settle its dispute with the union. It is difficult to say to what extent ancillary industry pressure may have contributed to AHP's decision to settle the RICO suits because other pharmaceuticals were, after all, AHP's competitors. There is, however, evidence to show that pharmaceuticals came together later as allies in 1993 to fend off the union's third Section 936 legislative reform bid. A later section in this chapter discusses the alliance of pharmaceutical interests that formed when the union convinced island interests that no Section 936 company would escape public scrutiny.

PERSONAL PRESSURE

Dual Pressures

OCAW used personal pressure tactics to cause AHP decisionmakers personal and professional embarrassment. This is not an uncommon corporate campaign tactic and it can take many forms.[47] Some of the "public pressure" tactics described above also had elements of personal pressure. Ths best example of this duality of intent was the Michael Moore visit and interview attempt. While

OCAW did intend for the company to receive negative publicity as a result of Moore's visit, they also hoped Moore would personally humiliate Whitehall managers on camera the same way he did GM executives in *Roger and Me*. The headquarters leafletting also had elements of personal and public pressure. While part of the union's goal was to foment internal dissent, it also wanted to remind managers of the consequences to workers of their corporate decisions.

July 1991 AHP Headquarters Protest

In July 1991, about three months before Whitehall-Elkhart was scheduled to close, 50 OCAW members traveled to New York to demonstrate in front of AHP headquarters and at board members' personal residences. These protests were the culmination of an intense period in the union's campaign. Only weeks before, Judge Pieras had ordered discovery to begin in the RICO I suit and AHP was facing the prospect of having to open its books to the union. Also, the Section 936 battle was heating up with Rep. Pete Stark's mid-June introduction of anti-runaway legislation in the House. Other pharmaceuticals were being drawn into the fray by publicity surrounding OCAW's list of 25 other "runaways" to Puerto Rico, and in Elkhart, AHP had just been prosecuted for federal labor law violations at a bitter and hostile NLRB hearing. Last, the union's publicity campaign seemed to be taking hold as national publications began to report on the situation.[48]

OCAW members spent a week in the New York area. On Monday, they demonstrated in front of company headquarters. They also let it be known to company officials that they would be there for a week. For the next three days, however, members visited the homes of top AHP officials and picketed and handbilled there. OCAW distributed handbills in the neighborhoods and at the workplaces of AHP officials and board members. They also leafletted chairman Stafford's country club parking lot.

At the end of the week, unionists returned to AHP's headquarters. This time they were met by police officers who ordered them to the other side of the street. Malloy and Local 7-515 steward Bernice Gilbert refused to move and informed the officers that they had picketed there on Monday without incident and without objection by the police. The police arrested the two women anyway for "disorderly conduct" as top company officials looked on from inside the building.

The women contacted LeRoy in Chicago who phoned a New York office of the American Civil Liberties Union (ACLU). An ACLU attorney immediately went to the police station and secured the unionists' release. Upon their release and to make the point that they would not be intimidated, Malloy and Gilbert returned to the headquarters and picketed for a few minutes directly in front of AHP headquarters. The union suspected AHP was behind the arrests (had AHP tried its own version of "personal pressure?"). Two months later a New York City judge dropped all charges against Malloy and Gilbert.[49]

Because of the substantive legal and legislative pressures the union already had in place at the time, the NYC demonstrations were particularly disturbing to some AHP officials who found them to be distasteful and offensive. Moreover, they lent credence to the general sense that the union would be ubiquitous and relentless in its campaign.

From the union's standpoint, the demonstrations solidified the resolve of union members to continue the fight, even as layoffs continued and the closure date approached. The visits to the homes of AHP officials revealed to union members the contrast between the futures they faced and the lifestyles the company would continue to provide its top managers after Whitehall-Elkhart closed. In the same way that a "picture is worth a thousand words," this image of juxtaposed, contrasting fates was powerful and motivated unionists to persist beyond even the plant closure.[50]

The arrests, however, posed somewhat of a public relations problem. As LeRoy pointed out, arrests are not in the union's interest because they "throw a wet blanket on organizing drives [and they] scare rank and file people."[51] As for the pickets at the residences, one school of thought says they are useless and counterproductive because they can create "an emotional enemy for life against the union."[52] This possibility was irrelevant to OCAW's decision to demonstrate in New York. The Whitehall closing would leave OCAW with no members at any AHP production facility in the world. The union did not have to consider the impact on future bargaining sessions with the company that might result from the pickets at officers' homes because there would be no more bargaining sessions.

The JTPA Hearings and the Value of Good Timing

Whether by design or luck or some combination thereof, OCAW employed its most significant personal pressure events to coincide with other substantive political or economic pressures. In the absence of these more substantive pressures, the personal diatribes would have been much less meaningful. As complements to other pressures, they were additive and helped to escalate the conflict. For example, the headquarters and home visits would have embarrassed and humiliated AHP executives even in the absence of the union's legal actions and Section 936 initiatives. But because OCAW pursued these powerful avenues of redress before it attempted to embarrass and humiliate the executives, it had armed itself to resist retaliatory actions by the company. Had OCAW only demonstrated and protested or done so before it had fortified its position, it seems likely that workers would have gained nothing. In fact, without the leverage of a lawsuit or the pressures of its assault on Section 936, the union may have received less than what it started with contractually because it would have had to engage in effects bargaining with AHP managers who were now "emotional enemies for life." Unarmed, the union's bargaining position would have been very weak.

Another case in point regarding the importance of timing to the efficacy of personal pressure tactics was the JTPA hearing in 1992. As Chapter Two explains, documents obtained in the RICO discovery led OCAW to believe that AHP fraudulently received federal monies under the Job Training Partnership Act (JTPA) to train some of its workers in Guayama. OCAW convinced Representative Tom Lantos (D-Calif.) to hold hearings on the matter.

In late April 1992, Judge Pieras set the trial date for the combined RICO suits to begin on August 3, 1992.[53] Fortunately for OCAW (but probably not coincidentally), Lantos scheduled the hearing for the week before the trial was to begin. Lantos subpoenaed Stafford on July 7 to appear on July 30, 1992 to testify before the House Employment and Housing Subcommittee of which Lantos was the chairman.[54] Ostensibly, according to Lantos' opening statement, the hearings were being held to examine "how on-the-job training (OJT) funds are being used, whether these funds are benefiting the economically disadvantaged and whether these scarce funds are being wasted."[55] Perhaps this was Lantos' priority, but OCAW had a different agenda in mind.

OCAW convinced Lantos that AHP received nearly a quarter of a million dollars in federal training subsidies and used those monies to hire and train for its Guayama, Puerto Rico plant, local workers whom they would have hired anyway. Moreover, the unionists said, these JTPA funds were a factor in the company's decision to operate in Puerto Rico and as such had "assisted in relocating [an] establishment...from one area to another," which was explicitly forbidden by the law.[56]

Union corporate campaigns often seek to uncover misuses of federal funds by the target company. This avenue provides opportunities for governmental intervention that would not otherwise be available.[57] When a company uses public funds (for example, for training or infrastructure development) it opens itself up to public scrutiny. Unions have few direct opportunities for adjudicative redress, the National Labor Relations Act being the most obvious exception, so they mount indirect challenges like OCAW's JTPA inquiry.

Lantos was the union's advocate and ally in these hearings. The subcommittee did not accuse AHP of violations of the law but of subverting the intent of the law and taking taxpayer money it did not need. During the course of the hearings, Stafford was put in the uncomfortable position of having to defend an AHP JTPA contract, albeit unfulfilled, "for ten chemist positions which require[d] a bachelor of science degree in chemistry, a chemist's license, and bilingual capability"[58] and for taking JTPA funds for "16 hours of training to show a high school graduate how to use a dust mop."[59] On the other hand, Lantos asked union representatives mostly rhetorical questions such as, "what is your opinion of using taxes paid from your own unemployment check to subsidize the wages of workers in another state who took away your job?"[60]

In many ways the 1992 JTPA hearing symbolized the entire Whitehall campaign. The unionists and their advocates raised many of the same issues at the hearing as they had raised throughout the campaign: the misuse of taxpayer dollars and of a federal program intended to create jobs, federal tax incentives as a driver of plant relocations, and collusion between AHP and Puerto Rico government officials to take advantage of a program to which the union claimed the company was not lawfully entitled. In a more general way, the hearing forum was itself metaphorical and symbolic of the corporate campaign construct. Here was a union confronting a corporation using a non-traditional tactic in an attempt to bring political, economic, legal and personal pressures to bear on corporate decisionmakers in order to change their behavior and redress the "injustice" of the corporation's actions. Here also was a well-orchestrated public relations event.

The JTPA hearing was an opportunity to present before the Congress all the issues the union thought were relevant to the Whitehall situation. The union had hoped all along for some kind of Congressional hearing in which it could expose AHP as "corporate outlaws" and demonstrate in a public forum the pain and casualties of the Whitehall shutdown. AHP knew that OCAW was behind the hearing and undoubtedly surmised that the questions would be lopsided. The company also knew that Stafford would have no choice but to sit there and answer them. As a personal pressure tactic, this is precisely what the union intended.

More than anything, the risks and costs of the impending RICO trial (and attendant negative publicity on the mainland and in Puerto Rico regarding Section 936) propelled the company toward a financial settlement with the union. The timing of the JTPA hearing to coincide with the onset of the RICO trial, however, added urgency to the company's movement toward resolution of the Whitehall matter and on July 27, three days before the JTPA hearing and six days before the RICO trial, the company settled with the union for $24 million. The JTPA hearing itself constituted remarkable personal pressure on Stafford. However, the timing of the hearing may have transformed it into pivotal pressure.

OCAW'S THIRD LEGISLATIVE DRIVE

"Our long struggle with American Home Products was just a part
of our larger struggle over Section 936 of the federal tax code. We
fully expect to continue if not redouble our efforts against the tax-
financed export of mainland jobs to Puerto Rico."

Robert Wages, president, OCAW-IU.[61]

When OCAW and AHP agreed on July 29, 1992 to settle the RICO suits, the parties also agreed to drop all other outstanding legal actions. This included OCAW's WARN suit appeal, arbitration proceedings over the company's decision bargaining obligation, an Equal Employment Opportunity Commission (EEOC) complaint the union filed in May 1992, outstanding NLRB matters, and AHP's suit against Stanley Fischer.

The company also demanded that OCAW "terminate its 'corporate campaign' against the company and...not encourage, promote or support any such campaign against the company."[62] While the settlement marked the end of OCAW's campaign on behalf of the Whitehall workers, it marked the beginning of the union's third legislative drive to reform Section 936.

60 Minutes and the AID

In the spring of 1992, prior to the settlement, OCAW began discussions with producers at the CBS television news program, *60 Minutes*, about an exposé on Section 936. At about the same time, other *60 Minutes* producers learned of another story about the U.S. Agency for International Development (AID) and its sponsorship of programs to promote the relocation of U.S. firms to Caribbean Basin production sites. Charles Kernaghan of the National Labor Committee (NLC) uncovered the story and brought it to the attention of the program producers.[63] The NLC had produced a report from AID documents which detailed the activities and expenditures this federal agency used to encourage companies in the U.S. to relocate to Central America to take advantage of very low wage rates there.

Two *60 Minutes* producers and Kernaghan posed as U.S.

businessmen interested in moving production from Miami to a site in El Salvador. On tape and on camera they recorded conversations with U.S. government officials who encouraged them to move and assured them that they would encounter no labor resistance due to a blacklisting sytem that operated to thwart union organizing activities. *60 Minutes* reported that the AID paid for promotional materials that advertised low wages ("You can hire [Rosa Martinez] for 57¢ an hour."), offered companies low-interest loans, subsidized worker training and the construction of production facilities. This story aired on September 27, 1992 and graphically illustrated how taxpayer-financed federal programs helped to displace American jobs. The OCAW-inspired Section 936 story never aired on the news program but the AID story explained briefly how Section 936 funds deposited in Puerto Rico banks were used to finance the establishment of off-shore low-wage production sites for U.S. firms.

The AID story made the union's point anyway; while firms naturally will seek to locate in the lowest cost production sites, the U.S. federal government should not promote the relocation of this production from U.S. facilities.

The impact and importance of this *60 Minutes* story to OCAW's third legislative drive cannot be overstated. The story aired only weeks before the presidential election and the media response was overwhelming. Within days, the ABC television news program, *Nightline,* covered the story for two successive nights with vice-presidential candidate Al Gore and Secretary of Labor Lynn Martin debating the accuracy and implications of the NLC revelations. Within weeks candidates Bill Clinton and Al Gore appeared on the talk show, *Donahue,* with laid-off workers from a AID-inspired shutdown and quoted details of the government's duplicity from the NLC report.[64] Over 100 newspapers across the country ran the story and Clinton and Gore made the federal sponsorship of job loss a primary campaign topic in the final weeks of the campaign. A Clinton pollster reported to Kernaghan that at one point in October, the issue of federally-sponsored, taxpayer-financed job loss was the issue about which Americans were the most concerned.[65]

This high-profile publicity although it did not focus only on Section 936, added to the growing public perception that the U.S. government was partly responsible for the loss of manufacturing jobs in the states. Vice-presidential candidate Al Gore took up the cause of a Decaturville, Tennessee manufacturer, which had moved its operations to Central America partially at the urging of the AID, and raised the issue during the vice-presidential debate. Vice-president Dan Quayle responded, "never have we ever, nor would we, support the idea of someone closing down a factory here and moving overseas."[66]

In addition to creating political heat at the height of the 1992 presidential campaign, the AID revelations inspired Congress to introduce legislation, within six days of the *60 Minutes* program, to prohibit the use of AID funds to promote the relocation of work from the United States to other countries.[67] The legislation was enacted shortly thereafter and it also prohibited assistance for "any project which contributes to the violation of internationally recognized workers' rights."[68] Similar language was adopted for the U.S. Overseas Private Investment Corporation (OPIC) and the Interamerican Development Bank.

This legislation was remarkable not only because it came about so quickly, but also because it clearly stated that U.S. taxes should not be used to finance the relocation of American jobs overseas. However, the rate of business relocations to these low-wage production sites is unlikely to end or slow as a result of these administrative changes because the fundamental economic advantage remains, even in the absence of U.S. promotional efforts. Also, subsequent agency guidelines seem to rule out only the most overt promotional and anti-worker activities and leave intact the institutions that have done the most to encourage relocations from the United States.

In spite of these shortcomings, this legislation directly attacked the federal sponsorship of job loss and thus was directly relevant to OCAW's final effort against Section 936. The publicity which propelled congressional action on the AID administration also enhanced the topicality of the Section 936 reform effort and sensitized lawmakers to the issue of taxpayer-financed runaways.

More Runaway Allegations

The election in November of Bill Clinton and Albert Gore to the White House signalled to 936-watchers that the tax law would receive serious scrutiny in the 1993 budget negotiations and proposals.

The 1992 Democratic convention discussions on the issue of Section 936 had revealed the Clinton administration viewpoint on this specific tax break, particularly to Puerto Rico supporters of the tax provision. Clinton and Gore's position on AID promotional activities left little doubt that federal programs like Section 936 would be targeted by the incoming administration. With two and a half years of publicity and Congressional lobbying as its foundation, OCAW intended to make runaways the driving issue behind Section 936 reform.

In the Whitehall campaign, OCAW used AHP to make its point about the job displacement effects of Section 936. Thus when it settled with the company, the union lost its most potent media angle. Section 936 was an arcane and complicated tax law and Puerto Rico did not figure prominently in the day-to-day concerns of the American public or their representatives in Congress. OCAW's use of AHP as a "runaway" example simplified the definition of Section 936, localized its consequences and thereby proved remarkably persuasive in attracting media and Congressional attention to the matter. However, the settlement precluded the further use of AHP as *the* "runaway" case in point. If the union's campaign and the issue of federal sponsorship of job loss were to continue to attract media attention, other runaway examples would have to be found.

Throughout the Whitehall campaign and especially after the 1992 election, the union made it known that it was looking for runaways to Puerto Rico.[69] OCAW leaders accessed the Federation for Industrial Retention and Renewal (FIRR) network and other activist labor organizations in its search. A FIRR affiliate in Tennessee provided OCAW the case it was looking for.

In late 1992, the Tennessee Industrial Renewal Network (TIRN) in Knoxville, Tennessee got wind of a potential plant closing at nearby Acme Boot in Clarksville. Acme was a subsidiary of Chicago-based Farley Industries, manufacturer of, among other products, Fruit of the Loom brand underwear and Dingo brand boots. A December article in *Caribbean Business* confirmed Acme Boot had applied for tax exempt status and planned to open a footwear assembly plant in Toa Alta, Puerto Rico that would employ about 250 people.[70]

The United Rubber Workers (URW) Local 330 represented the workers at Acme in Clarksville and leaders there were anxious to do whatever they could to save their members' jobs. In early January

1993, TIRN leaders arranged a meeting between the local URW executive board and LeRoy to discuss the possibility of mounting a campaign to avert the Acme plant closure. URW leaders were enthusiastic and soon thereafter engaged the services of both LeRoy and Leonard. The URW local contracted with LeRoy and the MCLR and Leonard worked with them on behalf of OCAW's Section 936 reform agenda.

The Acme situation offered real possibilities for the Section 936 campaign. First, the plant was not slated to close until May 1993. The five-month lead time gave union leaders time to develop and implement a shutdown aversion strategy. Compared to the 13-month lead time OCAW had for its Whitehall campaign, five months was not much time. However, the URW benefited by the campaign already in place. Also, OCAW considered this to be a runaway-in-progress so it could be targeted for administrative and legal challenges. These challenges also could be used as public relations fodder. Third, as in the Whitehall campaign, local union leaders were motivated to fight the plant closure and willing to use union funds to do it. Moreover, URW leaders and workers were willing to fight to reform Section 936 even though they knew that effort would not be likely to save their jobs. The national URW was supportive as well although it did not contribute financially to the campaign.

In some ways the Acme situation was even more compelling as a "runaway" example than was Whitehall. First, the Acme workers earned only $7.95 per hour. If even low-wage mainland jobs were not safe from the incentive effects of Section 936, what did that portend for the future of any manufacturing job in the states? Also, unlike AHP, Farley executives admitted to their employees in writing that they were moving Clarksville operations to Puerto Rico.[71] They denied, however, that this action was illegal and said they would move boot production out of Tennessee anyway.[72] Also, Puerto Rico had not yet granted Acme tax exempt status so an opportunity existed for the unions to prevent the tax grant through the forum of a Fomento administrative hearing. The unions saw more promise for an Acme hearing than they did in the AHP situation mostly because Fomento administrators responded immediately to the unions' request for an investigation into the matter.[73]

OCAW continued to look for other "runaway" cases even as it

worked on the Acme situation. In early 1993, OCAW turned up three possible candidates, a Syntex plant in Palo Alto, California,[74] a Colgate-Palmolive plant in Jersey City, New Jersey,[75] and a Sundstrand facility in Brea, California.[76] These cases escalated the pressure on island officials to take action on the mainland job relocation issue.

At Sundstrand, workers were represented by the United Auto Workers (UAW) union. OCAW learned of the Sundstrand situation in February as it helped FIRR update its third annual "Plant Closings Dirty Dozen" list. Fomento granted Sundstrand tax-exempt status only months before in December 1992, during a year-end rush to "get out pending cases" before the Hernández Colón administration left office. A record 53 tax exemptions were signed that month. The UAW attempted to compel Fomento to revoke Sundstrand's tax exempt status. Prior to its December 1992 tax grant, Sundstrand operated in Santa Isabel, Puerto Rico under a Westinghouse grant, whose electrical systems division Sundstrand bought in early 1992.[77] Although local UAW leaders challenged Sundstrand's tax grant application in Puerto Rico, they chose not to actively participate with OCAW in its broader Section 936 reform effort.

At Syntex, the workforce was not unionized and although the company publicly announced that it eventually would "shift all drug production for the U.S. market to its facility in Puerto Rico," OCAW found it impossible to organize resistance to the move among the workers there.[78]

In the Colgate-Palmolive case, the alleged production transfer from New Jersey to Puerto Rico was indirect and circuitous and had happened over a period of years beginning in 1988. "Not one job that ever existed in the United States is being done in Puerto Rico today," countered a Colgate-Palmolive spokesman.[79] The complexity of the production transfer allegation made it an unlikely candidate for even a Fomento challenge.

Although these three cases did not prove to be substantive opportunities to avert a mainland plant closing, they did help to create an impression in Puerto Rico that the island's tax grant program was under seige by mainland organized labor. In a March 1993 cover story, a *Caribbean Business* headline asked, "Runaway plant panic: Are labor unions the biggest threat to 936?" The story featured an interview with the acting director of Fomento who lamented, "the runaway challenges are the latest trend. What we are seeing is totally abnormal. So far this year, we've received four challenges, whereas in the 10 preceding years, we had seen only one complaint, the American Home Products case." Leonard claimed this onslaught was the result of "a growing anti-runaway grassroots movement here in the states."[80] The emerging legislative battle in Washington added weight to his admonition.

OCAW's Lobby for Support in the House

President Clinton's first State of the Union address in January and his subsequent budget proposal days later launched the official Section 936 reform effort in 1993.

> " . . . the tax code should not express a preference to American companies for moving somewhere else, and it does in particular cases today."[81]

His *Vision of Change for America* budget proposal gave form to his words by calling for a 65% credit on wages paid in Puerto Rico. This was a fundamental departure from the existing credit which was based on income earned by Puerto Rico subsidiaries. A wage credit would reorient Section 936 benefits to favor labor intensive firms and was designed to raise about $7 billion in new tax revenues from Section 936 corporations. Like the 1982 and 1986 amendments to Section 936 which increased the "active income" requirements, the wage credit was intended to promote island employment by essentially rewarding firms that hired the most people. The existing system favored capital intensive firms, like pharmaceuticals, and these firms stood to lose the most not only because the tax credit would be worth 65% rather than 100%, but also because it would be based on wages rather than income. OCAW favored Clinton's proposal but wanted a provision that specifically denied the credit to runaway firms; this was the goal of the union's legislative reform effort in 1993.

Clinton's budget bill was the obvious vehicle for specific anti-runaway legislation and because revenue bills begin in the House, OCAW focused its lobbying effort there first. National organized labor was solidly with OCAW on the Section 936 issue and had been for some time as demonstrated by the unanimous AFL-CIO Council Resolutions in 1992 and 1993 urging Congress "to deny this tax break to companies that would use it to shut down U.S. factories and transfer jobs."[82] Section 936 was virtually the only tax law in the Clinton budget proposal associated with a significant labor issue and its singularity helped concentrate the AFL-CIO's institutional support throughout the budget process.[83] The AFL-CIO's support remained solid because OCAW did not propose legislation that directly cut back Section 936 benefits. The AFL-CIO had affiliate unions in Puerto Rico and had to avoid the perception that it favored mainland workers over workers in Puerto Rico. As a result, OCAW's legislative proposals in the 103rd Congress did not expressly call for the elimination or even the reduction of Puerto Rico's tax advantages but rather sought to deny these benefits to runaway firms.

OCAW convinced three House members to introduce anti-runaway legislation. In early March, Rep. Fortney "Pete" Stark, D-California, reintroduced his 1991 bill that would deny Section 936 tax benefits to firms whom the Department of the Treasury determined were runaways to Puerto Rico.[84] Like the first bill, this was assigned to the House Ways and Means Committee, of which Stark was a senior member. Rep. Tim Roemer, D-Indiana, again co-sponsored the bill which differed only slightly from the original bill. Roemer also introduced legislation to amend the Worker Adjustment and Retraining Notification (WARN) Act to require companies with Section 936 subsidiaries to notify the Treasury Secretary of the closure, presumably so the federal government could watch for expansions or relocations in Puerto Rico by the closing company.[85]

On April 1, yet another senior House member joined OCAW's congressional anti-runaway campaign. Rep. George Miller, D-California, introduced a bill [86] that would change Puerto Rico law to prevent the island government from awarding runaway firms local tax exemptions. These exemptions lowered the amount of island taxes firms paid and were necessary for firms to be eligible for Section 936 benefits. Miller's bill did not seek to amend Section 936 but rather the Federal Relations Act which governs the island's relationship with the United States. Miller's legislation required Puerto Rico to obtain a sworn statement from each new company on the island certifying that it was not a runaway from the states. It allowed any entity that suffered economic injury, including state and local governments and labor unions, to sue the alleged runaway firm in federal court to recover compensation. Puerto Rico government officials would be immune from prosecution only if they obtained the sworn statements.

Miller's bill was more threatening to Puerto Rico than Stark's or Roemer's legislation. While Stark and Roemer proposed to amend the U.S. tax code, Miller's legislation proposed to amend the Federal Relations Act and to change Puerto Rico law. The Federal Relations Act is the law which established the island's Commonwealth status and as such is the fundamental legislative definition of the political relationship between the U.S. federal government and the Puerto Rico government. Advocates of Commonwealth status argue that the Act ensures Puerto Rico control over its internal political affairs because it was approved "in the form of a compact" and as such, requires the consent by Puerto Rico of any amendments to it. The Federal Relations Act never had been amended directly without Puerto Rico's consent, although Stark's 1985 legislation to cap Puerto Rico's rum excise tax rebates did abrogate one of its provisions.[87]

OCAW approached Miller about sponsoring a bill, and although he was receptive to the union's concerns, it would be months before he introduced his legislation. Miller was the chairman of the House Natural Resources Committee which oversaw legislation and other matters related to Puerto Rico. The island press reported that Miller was "no sympathizer of commonwealth status"[88] and the largest union in Miller's district was an OCAW local. Also, Miller was a friend to organized labor[89] and took the runaway plant issue "very seriously" because his district recently had lost many jobs due to defense cutbacks.[90] OCAW suggested the Federal Relations Act approach although its knowledge of the Act was informed by the Puerto Rico statehood advocates who had assisted the union throughout the AHP campaign. The statehooders' interest was obvious; if they could demonstrate that the Congress would amend unilaterally the Federal Relations Act, this would be "certain to weaken the public's faith in Commonwealth status as a special relationship."[91] OCAW, on the other hand, was interested in the political ramifications of an amendment to the Act because it further escalated the pressure for action on runaways to the island.

In March and April, both the House Ways and Means

Committee and the Senate Finance Committee held hearings on the Section 936 reform proposals.[92] The 1993 hearings for the most part mirrored the 1992 House hearings; the witnesses represented many of the same organizations and points of view. However, the intervening year had given both sides time to fortify their arguments with studies and statistics and a broader picture emerged of the costs and benefits of Section 936. Also, because witnesses testified on the president's specific 65% wage credit proposal, more of the 936 defenders' testimony spoke to the quality of jobs created by the current income credit and argued that a wage credit would make Puerto Rico just one more low-wage production location. They argued that the income-based credit brought high-tech, relatively high-paying jobs to the island and was responsible for creating (what there was of) a middle class in Puerto Rico. Opponents of Section 936, on the other hand, presented a very compelling and practically indisputable example of a runaway in the case of Acme Boot and showed how mainland workers, no matter how much they offered in wage and benefit concessions or how productive they were, simply could not compete with the financial advantages afforded by the tax credit.

Apparently, the latter argument was more persuasive in the House Ways and Means Committee. On May 13, 1993, the committee went even further than the Clinton budget proposed and passed a 60% wage credit and, more significant for OCAW, attached to it a specific runaway prohibition. Any analysis of this committee vote requires speculation and some reliance on hearsay and press accounts that quote anonymous lobbyists. Despite these caveats, there are some explanations which seem consistent with public testimony or were suggested by knowledgeable sources independent of one another.

As Chapter Two discussed, Rep. Charles Rangel, D.-New York was a long-time friend of and advocate for Puerto Rico and Section 936 partly because many of his constituents were of Puerto Rican descent. Union lobbyists counted him as the biggest obstacle in the House to reform of Section 936 due to his seniority and influence on the House Ways and Means Committee. In 1991 and 1992, Puerto Rico's governor and representative in Washington were united in their opposition to OCAW's Section 936 reform efforts. The 1992 election brought to power the PNP or statehood party, and although the new governor, Pedro Rosselló, advocated statehood, he vowed during his campaign to defend Section 936 so long as Puerto Rico was a commonwealth.[93] However, the island's new resident commissioner in Washington, former governor Carlos Romero Barceló, opposed Section 936 and announced early in the 1993 that he would not join in a campaign by Puerto Rico to save the tax credit.[94] Some analysts suggest that this disunity and polarity of viewpoints among Puerto Rico's top political leaders undermined Rangel's willingness to defend vigorously Section 936 during the committee's mark up of Clinton's bill.[95] Others attribute the Ways and Means Committee approval of the anti-runaway measure to vote trading by Rep. Andrew Jacobs, Jr. D.-Indiana, and to the support by Rep. Donald Sundquist, R.-Tenn. whose district included Clarksville, home of Acme Boot.[96] Surely, the combination of these influences is most explanatory and demonstrates again the breadth of interests the union had to invoke to succeed legislatively.

The *"Court of Public Opinion"*
OCAW's legislative effort benefited enormously by its very effective public relations campaign. The union built on the political momentum created by the Clinton budget proposal and combined it with the tragedy of the Acme situation to create an irresistible media story. For example, the union leaders were instrumental in bringing the Acme situation to the attention of an NBC television affiliate in Nashville, Tennessee. The station subsequently produced a news documentary called "Booted Out" about the Acme situation and its connection with Section 936. Soon thereafter Vice-President Al Gore (from Tennessee) took an active interest in the Acme case. The union attributes the initiation of this interest to the "Booted Out" documentary.

Media organizations and the public were primed to the issue of federal sponsorship of job loss in the U.S. thanks to the publicity it received during the presidential campaign. In the six months leading up to the votes in the House Ways and Means and Senate Finance Committees, OCAW drew coverage from some of the nation's most influential newspapers and by the some of the most widely-watched television news programs.[97]

OCAW's influence on the substance of the coverage can be

measured by the frequency of the appearance in these stories of Acme Boot as a runaway case-in-point and of LeRoy or Leonard as spokesmen for "organized labor's" anti-runaway campaign. The publicity surrounding the Acme situation ultimately forced Acme to withdraw its application for tax exemption just days before the House Ways and Means Committee voted on the Section 936 reforms. Fomento Administrator Clifford Myatt explained that the "union ha[d] been so vociferous and unfair in its attack on them that they [at Acme] [didn't] want any more bad PR."[98] This was a limited victory for the unions since Acme's application withdrawal did not preclude the closure of the Clarksville plant in Tennessee. Moreover, Acme could re-apply for Puerto Rico and Section 936 tax breaks at a later date. Acme's withdrawal did not hurt the union's publicity effort, however. In fact it may have added weight to the story since the tax grant application withdrawal was unprecedented and looked like an admission of guilt. Undoubtedly, a hearing, too, would have provided ample publicity opportunities, especially if Puerto Rico determined Acme to be a runaway and denied them the tax exemption. The withdrawal, though, fortified the Acme workers' position on the moral high ground and substantiated their contention that Section 936 was responsible for the Clarksville closure.

In 1993, OCAW worked exclusively on legislative remedies to Section 936-induced runaways and invoked the "court of public opinion" as its primary power base rather than the court of law as it had done earlier in the case of AHP. The *60 Minutes* story demonstrated the real political influence of a well-placed and -timed national news story and because the union's fight in 1993 was primarily a political one, OCAW directed significant resources to drawing the attention of large, national news organizations. This tactic was really the union's only viable option given the political weakness of organized labor in the U.S. at the time. Some Section 936 supporters attributed Congressional support for the anti-runaway amendment and Section 936 reform to a fear by some members of losing union support in subsequent elections.[99] This explanation was a misjudgment. Less than a year later this same Congress approved the North American Free Trade Agreement (NAFTA) and failed to pass a bill to prohibit striker replacements, two pieces of legislation considered much more important   to   national   organized   labor   than

Section 936 reform. If Congressmembers were afraid of labor as a voting constituency, it would have shown up here because national labor leaders explicitly threatened retaliation at the polls for wrong votes on these bills. Assuming fear was a factor at all, it is more likely that Congressmembers feared labor's (i.e., OCAW's) by now demonstrated ability to cast Section 936 supporters as proponents of huge tax giveaways to rich corporate giants at the expense of middle-class, family-wage jobs in the States. This characterization held greater potential for damage at the polls than did a threat of union voter retaliation.

The Puerto Rico Lobby to Save Section 936

Clinton's proposal to scale back Section 936 benefits caused political and business leaders in Puerto Rico to set aside their differences on the island's status and rally to the defense of the tax break. This effort ultimately encompassed Puerto Rico politicians of every party affiliation, business associations, industry lobbyists and leaders, newspapers, and even labor unions. It involved mainland politicians of Puerto Rican descent at the local, state and federal levels, especially in and around New York. The campaign was financed and advised by business and political associations in Puerto Rico, pharmaceutical and other industry consultants, and the Puerto Rico government. The campaign spent millions of dollars on its attempt to convince the U.S. Congress and president that a significant cut in Section 936 benefits would be disastrous for Puerto Rico's economy and would throw hundreds of thousands of Puerto Ricans out of work and force them to migrate to the mainland for jobs.

Some argue that this was not "Puerto Rico's" campaign but was instead an effort led by powerful Section 936 industry lobbies on the island and that Puerto Ricans were merely the "front men" of the operation. For the sake of simplicity, here it is referred to as the Puerto Rico/936 industry lobby. A thorough review would clarify the reality of the campaign but such a review is beyond the scope of this study. However, excellent starting points for this analysis may be found in two newspaper articles, one in *Caribbean Business* entitled, "Rallying the forces: Story behind the rescue of Section 936,"[100] and the other in the *Wall Street Journal* entitled, "How drug firms saved Puerto Rico tax break after Clinton attack."[101] These articles spell out the island

and mainland political and institutional influences that were brought to bear in this last-ditch effort to save Section 936. A full analysis would be a fascinating and illustrative case study of the machinations of American politics in the late twentieth century.

Several points must be made here, however. First, the Puerto Rico/936 industry lobby started to show its influence only after the House Ways and Means Committee voted to cut Section 936 and approved the runaway prohibition. Up to that point, the lobby's influence was frustrated significantly by Puerto Rico's resident commissioner in Washington, Romero Barceló, who refused to support the effort to preserve Section 936. This dissonance among Puerto Rico's top politicians made it difficult for legislators, except those familiar with the personalities involved, to discern what the Puerto Ricans wanted for themselves. It was not until the Senate Finance Committee hearings that island politicians started to demonstrate even the appearance of a united front. "I want to say it here clearly that I support whatever the Governor of Puerto Rico submits," testified Romero Barceló.[102]

The Senate Finance Committee was a friendlier venue for the Puerto Rico/936 industry lobby point of view than was the House Ways and Means Committee. The most important difference was the presence and chairmanship of Sen. Daniel Patrick Moynihan, D.-N.Y. Moynihan was somewhat of a scholar of Puerto Rican history dating back to the time when he was U.S. Ambassador to the United Nations during the Ford administration. In that position, he defended the island's Commonwealth status during U.N. decolonization hearings against Cuban charges that Puerto Rico was really a U.S. colony. Also, as a senator from New York, he represented over two million members of the mainland Puerto Rican diaspora for whom the island's economic condition remains a priority. Moynihan's knowledge about Puerto Rico's history and economy perhaps made him more receptive to the viewpoint that a sudden, radical shift in Section 936 benefits would create serious economic problems for the island. The press reported that Moynihan also worried that a big cut in Section 936 would skew the results of the upcoming status referendum set for November of that year.[103] On the other hand, Moynihan generally did not advocate tax incentives to promote economic activity, "you want to keep to an absolute minimum the amount of economic behavior that is tax-driven."[104] Given these counterbalancing beliefs it is not surprising that he advocated a compromise which mitigated the cuts approved in the House but still reduced Section 936 benefits significantly.

Of course, Moynihan was not the only influence on the content of the Senate bill. Sen. William Bradley, D.-New Jersey, also was positioned to play a determinative role in the outcome of the 936 tax reform. Bradley, the senior senator from New Jersey, was the fourth-ranking member of the Finance Committee. Bradley was viewed as an expert on tax issues and had criticized and even suggested the elimination of Section 936 in years prior to the 1993 debate. In 1992, it was rumored he would introduce legislation to reform Section 936 but that bill never materialized.[105] While Bradley may have viewed the incentive as problematical from a budgetary standpoint, his state also was home to a large concentration of major pharmaceutical companies. Bradley narrowly escaped defeat in the 1990 senatorial election and some analysts suggested that he needed the continued support of these powerful and heretofore generous constituents.[106] As Moynihan worked to preserve the size of the credit, Bradley's apparent priority was to maintain the credit as income-based. Pharmaceuticals stood to lose more than any other industry group if the credit were to be based on wages paid, as the Ways and Means Committee bill proposed.

Sen. David Pryor, D.-Ark. stood opposite Moynihan and Bradley on the Section 936 issue. Pryor had established himself as the public enemy of Section 936 years before the 1993 initiative. Pryor's priority, however, was to deny Section 936 benefits to drug companies. Pryor was the chairman of the Senate Special Committee on Aging and as such sought to protect senior Americans from the economic hardship caused by rapidly increasing prescription drug prices.[107] He had introduced several pieces of legislation over the years, including in 1993, to reduce significantly[108] or repeal entirely Section 936 benefits.[109] Pryor enjoyed a close political and personal association with President Clinton perhaps due to their years of public service together in Arkansas, and supported the president's proposal to change Section 936 to a wage credit. He also was the most publicly outspoken senator with regard to the disproportionate tax benefits pharmaceuticals received under Section 936. Beyond these issues, however, Pryor refused to involve himself with any other effect of the tax law. As a result, OCAW could not count on his support for its anti-runaway measure. The union's media campaign benefited enormously, however, by Pryor's virulent attacks on both the tax law and the pharmaceutical industry.

OCAW's Lobby of the Senate Finance Committee

After the House bill passed with the runaway provision intact, OCAW had two more legislative obstacles to overcome before the provision could become law. The first was the Senate Finance Committee. Everything that had gone right for OCAW in the House Ways and Means Committee went wrong for the union in the Senate Finance Committee. OCAW's priority was the anti-runaway provision, and union leaders found it impossible to convince any Finance Committee members to take up this cause in a meaningful way. Many of the union's natural allies were some of the same senators who were working to preserve the tax credit. Bradley, a Democrat with traditionally strong labor support, also was "typically the Senate's preeminent tax reformer."[110] He paid lip service to the union's cause but did little substantively to help until a young union official from a small OCAW local in New Jersey began to complain publicly and to other unionists in the state that Bradley was on the wrong side of the issue. Finally, after the House bill was out of committee, Bradley assigned an assistant to determine whether a runaway provision was viable.

Another likely ally of OCAW on the Finance Committee, Sen. Donald Riegle, D.-Michigan, demonstrated ambivalence toward OCAW's Section 936 reform effort. Some attributed Riegle's ambivalence to his Puerto Rican brother-in-law. OCAW enlisted the help of the United Auto Workers in Michigan to garner Riegle's support but to no avail. By chance, OCAW ultimately did receive some assistance from the senator. In June, a Riegle aide was scheduled to speak before a small OCAW local in Michigan but the aide never appeared. OCAW's Section 936 lobbyist took advantage of the opportunity to insist Riegle atone for the political blunder by helping the union succeed with its anti-runaway provision. With only weeks remaining until the Finance Committee vote, a Riegle aide who happened to be a tax attorney began to work with OCAW and Bradley's aide on the details of the anti-runaway measure.

The group arrived at a proposal that spelled out just how the Department of the Treasury would determine whether a new plant or expansion in Puerto Rico was a runaway. This was to be a new and unprecedented function for Treasury and ultimately department leaders were skeptical of the proposed determination process. The process was inherently political; one person's "runaway" was another's "corporate restructuring," and Treasury apparently wanted no part of it.

It was clear to the union that the Senate would not cut back the amount of the credit as much as the House had. The House bill sought to raise over $7 billion in revenue by the Section 936 tax increase but it looked as if the Senate would seek to raise much less than that and phase in the increases over a period of years. What was less clear was whether the Senate would retain the wage credit or revert back to the credit on profits. The weeks between the House and Senate votes saw intense campaigning by the Puerto Rico/936 industry lobby. Drug companies were at the forefront of the campaign and exercised their considerable financial and political influence in a final attempt to preserve the profits-based credit.[111] Meanwhile, OCAW held out hope that its final public relations push would compel the Senate to hold the line on the wage credit and include a specific anti-runaway provision.

In late May, *The Cronkite Report* aired a special one-hour program entitled "Help Unwanted" which documented the Acme Boot closure and the Section 936 tax break. The program was followed by an interview by Cronkite with President Clinton on these topics and the Acme situation in particular during which Clinton explained that his administration wanted to get rid of incentives for companies to move "overseas" and to give incentives to "stay here and modernize." Then, in late June on the night before the Senate Finance Committee was set to vote, ABC's *Primetime Live* aired a segment on Section 936 that was highly critical of the tax break and of the companies, especially pharmaceuticals, who took advantage of it. The program featured the Acme situation along with the pharmaceutical industry's nemesis, Sen. David Pryor, who slammed Section 936 as "the mother of all tax breaks." OCAW had worked hard to make these programs happen and hoped this national exposure and high-level publicity would fortify the senators' ability to resist the entreaties of the Puerto

Rico/ 936 industry lobby. Unfortunately for OCAW, this was not to be.

The Senate Finance Committee voted June 26, 1993, to retain the profits-based credit as well as a wage credit, giving companies a choice between the two. Also, the committee did not include a provision to prevent runaways. It did cut the income credit substantially however, allowing only a 60% credit on profits in 1994 which declined annually over five years until 1998, when companies would be allowed to take a credit against only 40% of their profits. The wage credit offered a 95% credit on wages paid.

OCAW had one final opportunity for its anti-runaway amendment by way of the House-Senate conference bill. The union's proposal to involve the Treasury was problematical and increasingly unlikely as the department grew more adamant in its resistance to the new responsibility. Only days before the House-Senate conferees wrapped up their work on the compromise bill, Treasury pulled out altogether. With no substantial leadership in the Senate on the matter of runaways to Puerto Rico and in the face of very formidable opposition in the person of Sen. Moynihan, the union held out little hope that either the House or Senate committee would force the responsibility on the Treasury. Thus, it scrambled to find another avenue by which the runaway provision could be included.

A Clinton administration official expressed a willingness to work with the union to see whether the Department of Labor would be a better home for the runaway determination responsibility. OCAW apparently had considered this option much earlier but decided against it. The Section 936 legislation was in the tax-writing committees in the House and Senate which had jurisdiction over the Department of the Treasury. Those committees did not have jurisdiction over the Department of Labor (DOL), however, and OCAW would have had to launch a parallel legislative effort in the labor committees in order to involve the Department of Labor in the runaway procedures. While the DOL may have been the natural home for the new runaway procedures, the details could not be worked out in time.

The Section 936 provision was only one of thousands of items under consideration in the 1993 budget bill. The House and Senate versions of the budget bill each passed by very narrow margins and the vote on the reconciliation bill was expected to be very close as well. The final weeks before the vote were a time of intense lobbying. In this period powerful and well-connected individuals and institutions could, because of their access and financial resources, affect the finer points of legislation. In this particular venue, OCAW's runaway provision stood little chance against the myriad and by now, well-coordinated forces of the Puerto Rico/936 industry lobby. OCAW could only speculate as to the specific sources of influence that convinced Treasury to refuse the runaway responsibility and there was little the union could do anyway to counter the department's resistance. It was unlikely that the union could invoke media interest in just one provision of a huge bill, so OCAW's most powerful tool to date was useless.

Only a powerful congressmember willing to make the runaway issue his top priority could have preserved the runaway provision at this late date. Such a member did not exist in the 103rd Congress. Thus, when Congress passed the Omnibus Budget Reconciliation Act of 1993 on August 5, 1993, it did not specifically outlaw runaways to Puerto Rico.[112]

The Final Legislation: Who Won?

The final Section 936 legislation was similar to the version which the Senate passed six weeks earlier. Section 936 firms were allowed to choose between either the wage or income credits. The only significant change was reflected in the wage credit provision. Now called the economic activity-based credit, it allowed a firm to take a 60% credit against its federal tax liability on the amount it payed in wages, fringe benefits, depreciation and Puerto Rican taxes. (The Senate version had allowed a 95% credit against wages only.) Under the income credit provisions, a firm could take a credit against its 1994 tax liability of 60% of its taxable income. This percentage declined five percentage points annually until 1998 whereafter the allowable credit against income was 40%.

Because the changes to Section 936 are so recent, whether these changes represent victory or defeat is a matter of perspective and interpretation. For Puerto Rican proponents of Section 936, the outcome represented an economic defeat but a political victory. Section 936 benefits were reduced significantly and many island leaders anticipate a rise in disinvestment as existing plants age, and a slowdown in new plants and expansions as the income credit continues to fall. Nevertheless, many islanders perceived the retention of the profits-based credit as an "heroic" achievement which demonstrated that Puerto Rico could play and win in the political big leagues.[113]

Pharmaceutical manufacturers will face a significant loss of tax benefits by 1998, assuming their capital/labor ratios stay the same. In fact, pharmaceuticals will pay most (about 67%, according to the Government Development Bank of Puerto Rico) of the new taxes collected under the revised rules.[114] On the other hand, Section 936 benefits were so generous to begin with that even a 60% reduction yields firms substantial tax benefits which are unavailable anywhere else in the United States. Furthermore, companies still receive a 100% credit on qualified possession source investment income, the passive income companies earn on their Puerto Rico financial investments. This incentive remains a lucrative and unique tax savings opportunity which will continue to operate as an inducement for U.S. companies to locate productive assets in Puerto Rico and elsewhere in the Caribbean.

Whether these assets will maintain current employment levels in Puerto Rico is open to question. Capital intensive firms will have less financial incentive to increase investment and production on the island. However, labor intensive firms there will have greater reason to stay and increase investment. Because of Puerto Rico's higher wage rate relative to other Caribbean locations, however, it is unclear whether the OBRA Section 936 wage credit will be enough to attract new jobs to the island. Time will show whether a shift from capital to labor intensive firms results in a net gain or loss of jobs for Puerto Ricans. Beyond the number of jobs, too is the question of the quality of jobs that will be retained or attracted to the island. Capital intensive firms, although they create few jobs, do tend to employ more highly skilled workers and thus pay higher wages per job than do labor intensive firms. Some analysts attribute the creation of a middle class in Puerto Rico to the concentration of capital intensive firms. Whether this "middle class" will expand because more Puerto Ricans are employed or decline because fewer of them earn high wages is unclear at this early date.

For OCAW and its organized labor allies, OBRA changes to Section 936 represent a significant reduction in the incentives that helped transfer thousands of jobs from the mainland to Puerto Rico.

However, those jobs already are gone and they are not likely to return to the mainland any time soon as a result of diminished Section 936 benefits. Nevertheless, if investment in Puerto Rico by capital intensive firms declines, then mainland workers may retain these jobs. The opposite also is possible, depending on the financial incentives of foreign production locations. Chapter Four discusses this issue further.

It is not entirely clear that the exclusion of OCAW's anti-runaway provision was a defeat for organized labor interests. This measure would have established a quasi-regulatory institution in the Treasury by which parties affected by a transfer of work to Puerto Rico could challenge the move in a public forum. OCAW demonstrated in its campaign to save Whitehall the importance of this sort of legal forum to groups who otherwise have no significant course of action. Such an institution, however, even as it was devised by OCAW, would not be free of problems for organized labor since the administrators of the institution would be political appointees. Thus, as in the case of the NLRB, the benefit to organized labor would depend on who held the White House.

Moreover, Puerto Rico has had an anti-runaway measure on its books since 1948. OCAW's campaign (and the fact that its Puerto Rico tax grant challenges were the first ever) revealed the impotence of such a regulation to prevent the transfer of work from mainland to island production facilities when the political will to enforce the law is absent. Also, JTPA and federal block grant abuses demonstrate the limited potential for work relocation prohibition clauses to prevent job shuffling. If organized labor continues to monitor new plants and expansions in Puerto Rico, this scrutiny will probably have a somewhat dissuasive effect on runaways, although challenges will be more expensive and time-consuming.

It is premature to evaluate the full impact of the 1993 changes on the tax expenditure level of the Section 936 credit. The periodic Treasury reports on the operation and effect of the possessions system of taxation on the federal budget typically lag three or four years, so the actual budgetary impact of the changes is as yet unknown.

As for the impact on the union and the company, OCAW reports it has lost no members to production transfers to Puerto Rico since OBRA was enacted. On the other hand, AHP recently announced it would close its Hammonton, New Jersey facility which manufactured some of the same products once produced in Elkhart and now produced in Guayama.[115] Hammonton was a nonunionized facility.

Why the Media Campaign Worked

OCAW's sophisticated public relations effort empowered the overall campaign and took it beyond the environs of the Whitehall plant and local community. It was fundamental to achieving the settlement and the legislative reform. There would have been little to publicize, however, had the union not undertaken the legal and legislative actions it did. Collective actions and interviews with destitute workers are only so newsworthy. The main issue could not be the plant closing. It had to be larger and relevant to the concerns of a wider audience. Only then could the publicity be transformed into commercial and political pressure.

It is important to point out, though, that the message alone did not create political pressure. The job displacement effects and disproportionate tax benefits of Section 936 were well-known (at least by some influential policymakers in Washington) for years prior to the Whitehall campaign. Only when OCAW objected and publicized these problems did Congress move significantly to ameliorate them. The combination of a compelling message and a sophisticated and powerful media effort made the difference.

The Whitehall campaign "had legs" because it showed "corporate welfare" in action. For now and the foreseeable future where job loss is at issue, as in a plant closing fight, the taxpayer connection and "corporate welfare" label will continue to be powerful rallying devices certain to garner not only media attention but also voter outrage and political action. One reason is that the argument against federal sponsorship of job displacement appeals to conservatives and liberals alike. In fact, one of the more ironic aspects of OCAW's campaign against federally sponsored runaway shops is that it was based on the same argument conservative economists and politicians used in the 1980's to thwart the creation of a Japanese-style, federally-directed "industrial policy." Then, conservatives contended that the federal government should not be in the business of "picking winners and losers" through tax subsidies and grants.[116] Also ironic; as President Clinton and the Congress denounced Section 936 (and earlier, AID incentives), they also proposed (and eventually instituted in OBRA 1993) the formation of federally-sponsored "economic empowerment zones." Under this federal program (which was enacted in the same legislation that reformed Section 936), states will receive federal subsidies and incentives to attract businesses to economically destitute (mostly urban) areas. The empowerment zone implementing legislation does contain anti-runaway-type provisions which forbid the use of these federal dollars to transfer jobs from one U.S. location to another. Nevertheless, the reality is, empowerment zone incentives are not in theory very different from Section 936 and every time the federal government spends money it influences investment decisions and thus employment location.

Thus, unless labor is willing to advocate the suspension of federal spending on job creation altogether, it will have to craft its message to the media to emphasize the impact of these expenditures on average working American taxpayers. The winner in the public forum will be the side that portends the greatest catastrophe or benefit to taxpayers of a particular policy change. One can only speculate as to the outcome of the Section 936 legislation had the Puerto Rico/ 936 industry lobby seriously attacked the reform as just one more Democrat-initiated tax increase.

NOTES

1   Edward S. Herman and Noam Chomsky, *Manufacturing Consent: The Political Economy of the Mass Media* (New York: Pantheon Books, 1988), pp. 33-34.
2   John Corry, *TV News and the Dominant Culture* (Washington, D.C.: Media Institute), 1986. Also, AHP officials interviewed for this study believed their side of the story was largely ignored by the media in favor of the more dramatic and politically shocking union story.
3   Herman and Chomsky propose a "propaganda model" which they claim has the effect of "filtering out" and "marginalizing" dissent. They "trace the routes by which money and power are able to filter out the news fit to print...and allow the government and dominant

private interests to get their messages across to the public." (Herman and Chomsky, *Manufacturing Consent,* p. 2.) If one accepts this premise, then OCAW leaders used this system of filters to their advantage and gained wide and sustained media coverage despite the fact that *they* were the dissenters.

4 Paul Jarley and Cheryl L. Maranto, "Union Corporate Campaigns: An Assessment," *Industrial and Labor Relations Review,* 43 (July 1990):5, p. 507.

5 For a variety of explanations and analyses of union corporate campaigns, see for example, Jarley and Maranto, *Union Corporate Campaigns,* July 1990; Charles Perry, *Union Corporate Campaigns* (Philadelphia: Industrial Research Unit, The Wharton School, University of Pennsylvania, 1987); Charles C. Heckscher, *The New Unionism: Employee Involvement in the Changing Corporation* (New York: Basic Books, 1988); Harold Datz, et al., "Economic Warfare in the 1980's: Strikes, Lockouts, Boycotts, and Corporate Campaigns," *Industrial Relations Law Journal,* 9 (1987):1 pp. 82-110; Dan LaBotz, "A Troublemaker's Handbook: How to Fight Back Where You Work and Win," (Detroit, Mich.: Labor Notes, 1991); Thomas A. Kochan, Harry C. Katz, and Robert B. McKersie, *The Transformation of American Industrial Relations* (New York: Basic Books, 1986).

6 Arnold Mayer, interview by author, 6 November 1994.

7 Midwest Center for Labor Research, "Social Cost Analysis of Possible Shutdown of Whitehall Laboratories, Elkhart, Indiana" (Chicago: Midwest Center for Labor Research), September 1990.

8 An employment multiplier was calculated using the data supplied by the U.S. Department of Commerce, Bureau of Economic Analysis. The methodology is described in *Regional Multipliers: A User Handbook for the Regional Input-Output Modeling System (RIMS II).*

9 Jim Miller, "Study: Whitehall shutdown would be 'devastating,'" *Elkhart Truth,* 6 September 1990 and Jeff Kurowski, "Union report sees dark days for displaced workers," *South Bend Tribune,* 6 September 1990.

10 Todd Dickard, "Group's work saved jobs in Buffalo," *Michiana Business Journal,* 7-13 September 1990.

11 Jim Miller, "Perron wins no promises from Whitehall officials,"
    Elkhart Truth, 5 June 1990 and Jeff Kurowski, "AHP links
    Whitehall fate to A.H. Robins acquisition," *South Bend Tribune*, 10
    May 1990.

12 Stephanie Davis, "Workers march for Whitehall jobs," *Elkhart
    Truth*, 4 September 1990 and Lelene Breckenridge, "Whitehall
    future still shrouded in mystery," *South Bend Tribune*, 4 September
    1990.

13 Locals 7-515 and 7-838 were the last remaining OCAW groups at
    AHP.

14 Jeff Kurowski, "Filmmaker on closing: there they go again," *South
    Bend Tribune*, 8 November 1990 and David Schreiber, "Moore
    urges Whitehall workers to fight back," *Elkhart Truth*, 8 November
    1990. OCAW arranged for a film crew from Chicago to accompany
    Moore in Elkhart.

15 Indiana newspapers in Anderson, Muncie, Ft. Wayne, Columbus,
    Michigan City, Marion, Gary, Madison, Warsaw, Bloomington, and
    Indianapolis ran the story. Also, a paper in Saginaw, Michigan
    covered it.

16 "Recession's Fellini," *The Economist*, 17 November 1990.

17 Jim Miller, "Whitehall union rallies for national support," *Elkhart
    Truth*, 4 October 1990.

18 Ibid.

19 Greg LeRoy, interview by author, 19 November 1994.

20 Ruth K. Thompson, "Union Use of Public Proxy Resolutions,"
    Labor Studies Journal, 13 (Fall 1988):3, p. 44. See also AFL-CIO,
    Industrial Union Department, *Developing New Tactics: Winning
    With Coordinated Corporate Campaigns* (Washington, D.C.:
    Industrial Union Department, AFL-CIO, 1985).

21 This resolution was drawn up by LeRoy and based on a similar
    resolution introduced in a Northern Telecom dispute.

22 Investor Responsibility Research Center, Inc., "Plant Closings and
    Dislocated Workers: American Home Products Corp.,"
    (Washington, D.C.: IRRC 1992 Background Report J, 31 March
    1992), p. 13.

23 Thompson, "Union Use," p.46.

24 AFL-CIO, *Developing New Tactics*, p. 28.

25 John O'Neill, "Union move on plant closings is defeated by stockholders," *The Wilmington Delaware News Journal,* 23 April 1992.

26 AFL-CIO, *Developing New Tactics,* p. 30.

27 Shortly after the Whitehall situation was resolved, AHP moved from its Manhattan location to a new suburban office complex in New Jersey. The new headquarters is virtually inaccessible to the public.

28 Harry Turner, "Union says pharmaceutical clearly was runaway plant," *San Juan Star,* 8 November 1991.

29 Stephanie Kohl,"Pickets warn of Whitehall layoffs," *The Press of Atlantic City (N.J.),* 13 July 1991.

30 "Whitehall closing New Jersey plant," *Elkhart Truth,* 20 May 1994 and "AHP eliminating 900 jobs," *South Bend Tribune,* 23 May 1994.

31 *Oil, Chemical, and Atomic Workers International Union v. American Home Products Corporation,* 91-1093 and 92-1238. (Plaintiffs' Memorandum in Support of Final Approval of the Proposed Settlement, p. 32)

32 Greg LeRoy, correspondence to author, 2 April 1995.

33 John Goff, "Flight fright at American Home Products," *Corporate Finance,* December 1990, pp. 42-44.

34 "AHP flap," *Corporate Finance,* April 1991, p.7.

35 Ibid.

36 Arnold Mayer, interview by author, 11 November 1994.

37 Harry Turner, "Indiana plant's move to P.R. becomes national issue," *San Juan Star,* 16 September 1991.

38 "La Fortaleza" refers to the Puerto Rico governor's administration. La Fortaleza is the governor's official residence.

39 Harry Turner, "Union charges pharmaceutical firm with 936 fraud," *San Juan Star,* 23 January 1991.

40 *Oil, Chemical, and Atomic Workers International Union v. American Home Products Corp.,* 92-1238. (p. 46)

41 "Union sues AHP for $1 billion in second suit," *Target Washington* (Washington, D.C.:bimonthly report on Puerto Rican affairs), 4:5, 6 March 1992.

42 Tom Bryan, "Union rejects runaway plants regulations," *Caribbean Business,* 12 March 1992, p. 20.

43 William Ruane, AHP Assistant General Counsel, interview by author, 21 March 1994.

44 Larry Rohter, "Puerto Rico votes to retain status as Commonwealth," *New York Times,* A, 1:6, 15 November 1993.

45 Larry Rohter, "Settling question of statehood tops agenda of new Puerto Rico governor," *New York Times,* A, 16:1, 18 December 1992.

46 "AHP 'runaway' to Puerto Rico spurs union lawsuit," *Health News Daily* (Chevy Chase, Md: Health News Daily), 3:15, 23 January 1991.

47 Perry, *Union Corporate Campaigns,* p. 61; Datz, et al., *Economic Warfare,* p.112.

48 Paul Glastris, "Pain relief," *U.S. News & World Report,* July 1, 1991; Merrill Goozner, "Elkhart American Home case sparks bill to cut tax credits," *Chicago Tribune,* 13 June 1991; Lawrence Henry, "The strange case of Section 936," *CFO,* May 1991.

49 "N.Y.C. judge drops union picket charges," *Elkhart Truth,* 4 September 1991.

50 LeRoy called the visits "incredible class-consciousness builders," (Greg LeRoy, correspondence to author, 2 April 1995) and Malloy reported that member morale improved significantly as a result of the visits and demonstrations. (Connie Malloy, interview by author, 28 April 1995.)

51 Jeff Kurowski, "Union leaders deny arrests intentional in Whitehall protest," *South Bend Tribune,* 14 July 1991.

52 Datz et al., "Economic Warfare, p. 113.

53 Harry Turner, "Union lauds early trial date set on 'runaway' plant cases," *San Juan Star,* 28 April 1992.

54 House Committee on Government Operations, Employment and Housing Subcommittee, *Waste and Misuse of Federal On-the-Job Training Funds,* 102nd Cong., 2nd session., 5 August 1992, p. 102.

55 Ibid., 30 July 1992, p. 1.

56 Ibid., p. 2.

57 Charles Perry, *Union Corporate Campaigns* (Philadelphia: Industrial Research Unit, The Wharton School, Univ., of Pennsylvania, 1987), p. 51.

58 House Committee on Government Operations, *Waste and Misuse,* 5

August 1992, p. 89.

59 Ibid., 30 July 1992, p. 2.

60 Ibid., p. 41.

61 Robert Wages, president of the OCAW-IU, as quoted by Tom Bryan and Pablo Trinidad, "Union swears anti-936 campaign will go on," *Caribbean Business*, 6 August 1992.

62 *Oil, Chemical, and Atomic Workers International Union v. American Home Products, Corp.* 91-1093 and 92-1238. (Settlement, p. 3-4.)

63 The full name of the National Labor Committee is the National Labor Committee in Support of Worker and Human Rights in Central America. The NLC was founded in 1980 and is a committee of 21 international unions, represented by their presidents.

64 "Clinton and Gore from Nashville," on *Donohue*, (New York: NBC, Multimedia Entertainment, Inc.), air date 6 October 1992.

65 Charles Kernaghan, interview by author, 3 January 1995.

66 "Quayle and Gore battle devolves into a hand-to-hand fight about 4 issues," *New York Times*, 14 October 1992.

67 Public Law 102-391, sec. 599.

68 *Congressional Record*, 102nd Cong., 2nd sess., 4 October 1992.

69 Harry Turner, "Union set to take more 936 firms to court," *Caribbean Business*, 19 November 1992.

70 Pablo Trinidad, "Acme Boot to produce footwear in Toa Alta," *Caribbean Business*, 10 December 1992.

71 House Committee on Ways and Means, *President Clinton's Proposals for Public Investment and Deficit Reduction*, 103rd Cong., 1st sess., part 2 of 2, 1 April 1993, pp. 1367-1373.

72 "Union attacks company on move to P.R.," *Target Washington* (Washington, D.C.: Target Washington), 5: 1, 8 January 1993.

73 Robert Friedman, "Acme Boot Company: A runaway plant?" *San Juan Star*, 10 January 1993.

74 Beatriz de la Torre, "Runaway plant panic: Are labor unions the biggest threat to 936?" *Caribbean Business*, 11 March 1993, p. 2.

75 Beatriz de la Torre, "U.S. unions, P.R. gov't fight over runaways," *Caribbean Business*, 4 March 1993.

76 De la Torre, "Runaway plant panic," pp. 2-3.

77 Ibid.

78 Ibid. and Richard Leonard, interview by author, November 1994.

79 De la Torre, "U.S. unions."

80 De la Torre, "Runaway plant panic."

81 William Clinton, *Vision of Change for America* (Washington, D.C.: GPO), 17 February 1993, p.104.

82 AFL-CIO Resolution, 22 February 1992.

83 Greg LeRoy, interview by author, December 1994.

84 H.R. 1210, 103rd Cong., 1st sess., 4 March 1993.

85 H.R. 1207, 103rd Cong., 1st sess., 4 March 1993.

86 H.R. 1630, 103rd Cong., 1st sess., 1 April 1993.

87 "Chairman Miller files runaway plant bill," *Target Washington* (Washington, D.C.: Target Washington), 5:8, 16 April 1993.

88 Harry Turner, "Congress proposes runaway plant bill," *Caribbean Business,* 15 April 1993.

89 Michael Barone and Grant Ujifusa, *The Almanac of American Politics* (Washington, D.C.: National Journal, Inc., Times Mirror Company, 1994), pp. 105-106.

90 Robert Friedman, "Congress zeroes in on 'runaways,'" *San Juan Star,* 12 April 1993.

91 Harry Turner, "P.R. hearing to be followed in Capitol," *Caribbean Business,* 29 April 1993.

92 House, Ways and Means, *President Clinton's Proposals;* Senate Committee on Finance, *Administration's Tax Proposals (Foreign Tax and the Possessions Tax Credit- Section 936 of the Internal Revenue Code),* 103rd Cong., 1st sess., 27 April 1993.

93 Rick Wartzman and Jackie Calmes, "How drug firms saved Puerto Rico tax break after Clinton attack," *Wall Street Journal,* midwest edition, 21 December 1993, p. A1.

94 Manny Suarez, "Gutierrez: CRB's failure to back 936 was irresponsible," *San Juan Star,* 27 February 1993.

95 Wartzman and Calmes, "How drug firms saved Puerto Rico," p. A4; Arnold Mayer, interview by author, January 1995.

96 Doreen Hemlock, "Battle lines form on 'runaway plants,'" *San Juan Star,* 15 May 1993.

97 CNN *Moneyline,* 22 January 1993; CBS News, March 1993; The Cronkite Report, 28 May 1993 (includes an interview with President Clinton on federal sponsorship of job loss); ABC *Primetime,* 24

June 1993; Daniel Southerland, "Clinton targets territories' tax break," *Washington Post,* 24 February 1993; *Wall Street Journal,* January 1993; *New York Times,* 3 January 1993.

98 Doreen Hemlock and Robert Friedman, "Acme Boot eschews tax breaks," *San Juan Star,* 7 May 1993.

99 Robert Friedman, "Future of 936 becoming dimmer," *San Juan Star,* 14 May 1993; Doreen Hemlock, "Labor flexes muscle in 936 debate," *San Juan Star,* 17 May 1993; Pablo Trinidad, "Labor stomps 936," *Caribbean Business,* 20 May 1993.

100 Pablo Trinidad, "Rallying the forces: The story behind the rescue of Section 936," *Caribbean Business,* 5 August 1993.

101 Wartzman and Calmes, "How drug firms saved Puerto Rico."

102 Senate Finance Committee, *Administration's Tax Proposals,* p. 7.

103 Wartzman and Calmes, "How drug firms saved Puerto Rico;" *New York Times,* 24 July 1993, I 26:3.

104 Barone and Ujifusa, *Almanac of American Politics,* p. 860.

105 Harry Turner, "Sen. Bradley drafts bill to halt 'runaways,'" *San Juan Star,* 31 October 1991.

106 Wartzman and Calmes, "How drug firms saved Puerto Rico," p. A4.

107 Julie Kosterlitz, "Jawboning with a bite: Chairman of Special Committee on Aging, David Pryor, attacks the pharmaceutical industry," *National Journal,* 24:21, 23 May 1992.

108 *Prescription Drugs Cost Containment Act of 1992,* S. 2000, 102nd Cong., 1st sess.

109 *New York Times,* 16 February 1993, D, 17:3.

110 Wartzman and Calmes, "How drug firms saved Puerto Rico," p. A4.

111 Ibid.

112 Public Law 103-66, Section 13266.

113 Trinidad, "Rallying the forces;" *Wall Street Journal,* 4 August 1993.

114 Doreen Hemlock, "Pharmaceuticals to bear bulk of new taxes," *San Juan Star,* 25 August 1993.

115 "Whitehall closing New Jersey plant," *Elkhart Truth,* 20 May 1994; "AHP eliminating 900 jobs," *South Bend Tribune,* 23 May 1994.

116 Congressional Budget Office, *Industrial Policy Debate* (Washington, D.C.: GPO), December 1983.

IV

Was It Worth the Fight?

This study analyzed how a small union transformed a "garden variety plant closing" into a national issue by exposing one way in which the U.S. federal government sponsors job loss in the United States. The union won a substantial $24 million settlement from the company in an unprecedented legal action and led a tax reform effort that resulted in one of the few meaningful legislative measures to address "runaway shops." While the union's achievements are remarkable, the fact remains that 800 people lost their jobs. This reality raises the obvious question; was it worth the fight?

Costs

The OCAW International Union spent roughly $1 million on the Whitehall campaign and Section 936 legislative reform effort.[1] The local union spent down its funds entirely, a total of about $25,000 during the course of the campaign.[2] Campaigns of this nature and extent are costly and such expenditures are not uncommon. Jarley and Maranto have reported that the "typical corporate campaign, as estimated in public reports...is about a million dollars per year."[3] Compared to this "typical" rate, OCAW's three-year, $1 million campaign seems to have been a bargain. However, corporate campaigns vary tremendously in their goals and tactics so that simple cost comparisons among them are probably not very meaningful. Moreover, however a campaign's cost compares to the norm, it is still an expensive undertaking, especially for a relatively small union like OCAW.

OCAW's successful media campaign helped to minimize costs while it maximized the impact of expenditures the union did make. Every news story that told OCAW's point of view was, in essence, free advertising. Also, OCAW held down its direct outlays in legal fees by enlisting its RICO suit attorneys on a contingency fee basis. Finally, OCAW enjoyed the benefit of thousands of hours of volunteer labor from its members in Local 7-515.[4]

The personal costs are more difficult to quantify but no less real. Union leaders spent untold weeks away from their homes and families, some over a period of nearly three years, with no certainty their efforts would pay off. Union members also devoted a tremendous amount of time and energy to the campaign before and after they were laid off. The fight delayed bargaining over an effects package with no guarantee that in the end, workers would receive any more benefits than they would have received without the fight. In fact, some workers legitimately feared that the campaign would anger AHP and cause the company to reduce severance benefits.

Benefits

Settlement. In July 1991, AHP and OCAW settled the RICO suits (and all other outstanding legal actions) for $24 million. As the union's attorney Alan Kanner pointed out at the conclusion of the settlement, "no other worker in a state of the United States ha[d] ever recovered one cent from an alleged 'runaway' plant."[5] Indeed, it was almost unheard of for any union anywhere in the United States to win anything in a plant closing battle. This was an historic outcome but was the campaign worthwhile to union members beyond its historical significance?

As Table 2 shows, on the whole, union members were better off financially with the RICO settlement payout than they would have been under the terms of their last contract. AHP maintains, however, that after the attorneys' fees, members got no more than they would have received had they simply bargained over the effects of the closure.

Nonetheless, there are some elements of the settlement which seem to go beyond normal effects bargaining terms; in particular, the settlement's three weeks' pay per year of service, $1.5 million

TABLE 2
Benefits Comparison

	For Terminated Class Members				For Local 7-515 Employees Transferring to Other AHP Plants[a]				For the OCAW-IU
	Severance Pay	Health Insurance Coverage	Education Scholarship Fund	Pension Eligibility	Severance Pay	Moving Expenses	Seniority Rights to Determine Benefits	Seniority Rights to Determine Layoffs	Funds in Excess of Whitehall Campaign Expenses
Settlement and Effects Bargaining Provisions	*3 weeks per year of service*[b]	*10 months*	*$1.5 million*[c]	*Everyone vested*	*1 week per year of service plus $500*	*$4,500*	*Retain*	*Lose*	*$1.0 million*
Contract Provisions	*1 week per year of service*	*4 months*	*None*	*Vested after 5 years' seniority*	*None*	*None*	*Lose*	*Lose*	*None*

---

[a] 52 transferred, 40 of whom were subsequently laid off.

[b] First two weeks severance pay based on an age/service formula to a maximum of 52 weeks. Every class member received a third week's pay. The total for all class members was roughly equivalent to three weeks' total pay per year of service.

[c] Funds available to workers and their immediate family members.

scholarship fund, and payment of moving expenses. A comparison of the severance benefits from another AHP closing around the same time is perhaps illustrative of the superiority of the Whitehall settlement.

In October 1993, AHP closed another unionized pharmaceutical plant in Windsor, Ontario. The union there, the Energy and Chemical Workers Union (ECWU), attempted to resist the shutdown but without success. The effects bargaining package the ECWU negotiated with AHP allowed only two weeks' severance pay per year of service, paid no moving or job search expenses, and curtailed prescription coverage (other health care coverage is provided by the Canadian government). The company provided scholarship money but only for one year after the plant closed.[6] At Whitehall, the $1.5 million scholarship fund was to be distributed over a three-year period, then, if a balance remained, it would be donated to a charity of the union's choice. Clearly, OCAW's severance benefits were superior to the ECWU's.

By way of further comparison, the periodic surveys of union contracts by the Bureau of National Affairs showed that in 1992 only 3 percent of union contracts allowed two weeks' severance pay per year of service and no contracts granted three weeks or more. Most contracts (77%) offered one week's severance pay.[7] While contract benefits are often not what unions end up with after an effects bargaining session, this comparison is a useful benchmark nonetheless and illustrates that the RICO settlement benefits were indeed out of the ordinary.

For comparative purposes, it also is worth noting that when non-unionized plants close, workers typically get little or nothing in the way of severance benefits or readjustment assistance. This is not necessarily the case, however, at non-unionized AHP facilities. OCAW and the ECWU report that AHP typically pays its non-unionized employees higher wages and provides them better pension, medical and severance benefits as a way of encouraging union de-certification and discouraging further unionization at its plants.

This being the case, it seems clear that unions at AHP facilities help set the benchmark wages and benefits for the entire corporation and that non- unionized workers there benefit from the wage demands of the few unionized AHP employees. If, as OCAW alleges, AHP succeeds in eliminating all unions from its production facilities, it will be interesting to see if wage and benefit levels change.

State and Federal Aid. Between September 1990 and March 1991, OCAW sought and secured nearly $1 million in federal and state grants to assist the laid-off Whitehall workers. The first grant underwrote a study by a Massachusetts-based FIRR affiliate, the ICA Group,[8] to study the possibility of an employee buyout or of finding a buyer willing to keep the business in Elkhart. However, AHP did not plan to exit the business it operated in Elkhart, it wanted to move it. Thus a buyout discussion was pointless. Moreover, AHP refused to cooperate because it thought the ICA Group was an arm of the union and would use the information it sought to further the union's campaign.[9] Ultimately, the ICA Group only studied and made recommendations for the sale of the empty Elkhart plant facility.

OCAW used the remaining state and federal assistance for retraining programs, job search and career counseling, peer counseling and child care and transportation to and from job training facilities. OCAW negotiated to use part of the funds to pay two ex-Whitehall workers full-time to act as peer counselors to ensure that workers took full advantage of the programs and funds available. Working with federally funded "private industry councils", the union established a program geared to the specific needs of the Whitehall workers. Also, Malloy convinced state regulators to qualify laid-off workers as "dislocated" even before the plant formally closed. This allowed the workers to take advantage of retraining programs before the company officially terminated them.

While $1 million seems like a significant amount of money, it worked out to only about $1,700 per worker, well below the $3,000 typically seen in similar shutdown situations.[10] LeRoy suggests that the main reason Elkhart workers received less than the average is because they were ineligible for trade-related adjustment assistance; although Whitehall production moved offshore it did not move to a foreign location.

Some of the funds would have been available to laid-off Whitehall workers even without the union's involvement. In a shutdown, the state agency which administers the disbursement of federal training funds is supposed to contact dislocated workers to make them aware of the assistance available. This is especially true in a situation like the Whitehall shutdown in which hundreds of workers at once faced layoffs and the company issued a WARN notification to the state. Nevertheless, recent studies show that the distribution and administration of federal and state retraining and readjustment assistance funding is uneven at best. A recent study by the U.S. General Accounting Office (GAO) counted 163 federal programs among 15 federal agencies that provide training assistance. This myriad of training and assistance programs can "confuse and frustrate clients, employers, and administrators."[11] OCAW worked through the tangle of programs and aggressively pursued the funds to which it was entitled. In so doing, the union ensured that its members had maximum access to government-funded opportunities for retraining and readjustment.

Beyond the acquisition of funds, the union also worked to ensure that the dollars were administered to the greatest benefit of the workers. The union assigned former coworkers to be the job search and training counselors rather than leave that responsibility to state employees. OCAW leaders believe union members consequently accessed the assistance more than they otherwise would have. The union also believes the assistance dollars were spent more efficiently and benefited the workers more; counselors felt a greater responsibility to workers whom they knew and worked harder to place them in good jobs instead of simply finding employment for them anywhere for any wage. In its recent study, the GAO characterized federal training programs as inefficient, inattentive to individual training needs, and lacking in administrative accountability.[12] To the extent that OCAW's hands-on involvement ameliorated these specific problems, it helped sidestep some of what undermines other readjustment efforts.

Legislative Gains

Beyond the AHP settlement, OCAW's campaign against Section 936 was a mission to eliminate the federal sponsorship of job loss. To this end, the significant reduction by OBRA 1993 in Section 936 benefits may slow the movement of production jobs from the states to Puerto Rico in capital-intensive industries. More taxes will likely be collected from pharmaceutical companies operating in Puerto Rico, assuming their capitol/labor ratios stay the same. In fact, pharmaceuticals will pay most of the new taxes collected under the revised rules, about 67% according to the Government Development Bank of Puerto Rico.[13]

OCAW did not achieve what it wanted most, however, namely an explicit legislative prohibition against runaways to Puerto Rico. The House of Representatives approved it but the Senate did not.

In conference, the Senate prevailed and the union was left to hope that the cuts to the income credit will mitigate the runaway problem. There is one element to the final legislation that may undercut and even backfire on the union's efforts, however.

OCAW attached its anti-runaway provision to the House proposal to change Section 936 to a wage-based credit. The wage-based credit was an attempt to make the incentive more efficient in terms of the number of jobs created per tax dollar spent. From a budgetary standpoint, the wage credit was logical. This was the only Section 936 legislation that stood a chance of passage at the time so the union had no choice but to try to attach its amendment to this bill. In addition to political considerations, OCAW and the AFL-CIO also were compelled to go along with the wage credit on philosophical grounds. As labor advocates, the unions had to support the wage credit because it would reward those firms in Puerto Rico that employed the most people rather than those that simply earned the most profits.

The final legislation, however, retained part of the income credit *and* allowed a wage credit. Firms choose which credit they want to take. Now, labor intensive firms have a greater incentive to locate production in Puerto Rico. Thus one could easily envision a scenario in which a new wave of labor-intensive firms moved from the states to Puerto Rico. This would be good for Puerto Rico in terms of employment and good for the federal budget deficit in terms of tax efficiency and reduced transfer payments to Puerto Ricans. Would it, however, benefit or hurt mainland workers?

One can argue (and some did during the debates over Section 936) that labor-intensive manufacturing is leaving the states anyway to very low-wage production sites in the Caribbean Basin, Mexico and Asia, and that Puerto Rico does not compete for those jobs, even with the wage credit. It seems reasonable to presume, however, that some companies that are looking to reduce costs through a production relocation would need or prefer Puerto Rican workers, who are English-speaking, relatively well-educated Americans, and need or prefer the economic and political stability that Puerto Rico provides. There are some labor-intensive companies, in other words, that would not choose to move production to a foreign country to take advantage of lower wage rates but would choose to move to Puerto Rico for its tax advantages. Therefore, the cuts in Section 936 and its reorientation to labor-intensive industries may not entirely curtail runaways or protect mainland jobs. The tax law changes are very recent and it is too soon

to know the extent to which the changes will affect the Puerto Rico and
mainland economies. It seems clear, however, that mainland organized
labor will have to continue to monitor the movement of work to Puerto
Rico and use the threat of a Fomento administrative appeal if it is to
entirely thwart runaway production.

AHP and Organized Labor

From the company's standpoint, the question, "was it worth the
fight", is practically moot. AHP had no choice but to engage in the
battle with OCAW. When OCAW sued the company or filed
complaints with the NLRB, it had to defend itself. When AHP's
chairman was confronted with questions from OCAW members at its
annual meetings, he had to answer them. When he was summoned to
Capital Hill to testify at the JTPA hearings, he was bound to appear.
However, to the extent that AHP could avoid the fray, it did so. AHP
took the offensive on very few occasions in its battle with the union and
instead simply moved forward with the shutdown schedule, responding
only when there was no alternative. OCAW would characterize the
company's response (or lack of it) as arrogant and evidence of its
historical proclivity to avoid publicity about any corporate matter. The
company would attribute its mostly defensive posture to its desire to
avoid beating up on workers whom they were about to lay off and to its
respect for organized labor generally. There seems to be evidence to
support both points of view.

"Arrogance" and Anonymity. An "arrogant" corporate
response would have to be founded in a sense of superiority. Indeed, the
company was superior to the union in several fundamental ways. It had
superior authority with regard to capital decisions and had at its
disposal vastly superior financial and organizational resources. These
advantages would lend confidence to any organization involved in a
dispute. In practical terms, this was not an even match and it is no
wonder the company underestimated the union's leaders and their ability
to mount a substantive challenge to the closure decision.

When Malloy started the campaign to keep Whitehall open,
she and a few union members represented the sum total of the
opposition. Malloy, a small, pretty, soft-spoken mother of two, belied
the traditional stereotype of a powerful union boss. Her persona and her
position as the leader of a small local union did little to arouse

concern among AHP officials that hers would be more than a cursory objection to the closure. Moreover, she was very new to the presidency and though she had won overwhelmingly, this electoral support did not necessarily guarantee membership loyalty, especially under the extreme stress of a plant closing battle. Thus, logic suggested a minimal response from the corporation, at least at the outset.

Some analysts characterize American Home Products' corporate "style" as low-key and averse to publicity. They point to the company's tradition of austerity and reticence with regard to the press. as evidence of a policy to avoid the spotlight.[14] Indeed, AHP had no corporate public relations staff until 1991, when the OCAW publicity began to take its toll on the company's image. This lack of a corporate public relations department was remarkable for a consumer products company the size of AHP. That AHP hired a vice president for public relations for the first time during the height of the Whitehall battle would seem to be evidence of the efficacy of the union's publicity campaign against the company.[15] AHP maintains, however, that this change was coincidental to the Whitehall campaign and reflected a general change in organizational priorities that came about with John Stafford's ascendency to the CEO position. Within months of the Section 936 cuts and the end of OCAW's runaway plant reform effort, AHP's new PR. man left the company and his responsibilities were integrated into a new position, vice president for investor relations.

During the Whitehall campaign, nearly all press inquiries were channeled to the corporate secretary whose responses typically were brief and noncommittal and expressed the company's desire to avoid fighting its battles in the press. Local reporters covering the situation estimate that the union's press releases outnumbered the company's by more than four to one.[16] The company attempted no public relations "damage control" measures until the union's campaign was nearly a year old. OCAW claims, however, that the company used more subtle pressure tactics, especially in the plant. The NLRB's rulings in the union's favor seem to bear out these claims. On the few occasions when the company did make overt efforts to create favorable publicity for its actions, they suffered from unfortunate timing or encountered union countermeasures.

In January 1991, for example, the company decided to donate the Whitehall plant to the city of Elkhart. AHP also agreed to pay for an environmental audit, for maintenance, utility and security costs for one year after the ownership transfer, and $75,000 in realtor fees to market the building. This was a generous offer but it happened to be announced on the same day the Gulf War began, so the story was subsumed. Even after, when the donation could have paid off in public relations terms, the company did not receive much credit. Instead, the mayor of Elkhart drew most of the kudos for having "convinced" AHP to make the donation.[17]

The facility donation did little to mitigate the union's attacks; only weeks later, OCAW filed the first RICO suit and the WARN suit. Also by this time, the NLRB had filed the complaints against the company and had set a hearing date. The Whitehall situation had become more than a minor annoyance to the company and AHP moved to erode support for the union's campaign among OCAW members in Elkhart.

In January 1991, AHP retained the services of Benchmarketing Associates, a local public relations firm in South Bend, Indiana. This new connection with Benchmarketing appeared to "represent an effort by AHP to improve the flow of information from the corporation."[18] At about the same time, AHP was in contact with The Kamber Group, a Washington, D.C.-based public relations firm. Kamber executives attended the OCAW press conference in Washington, D.C. at which the union announced its first RICO suit.[19] When it became clear to OCAW that the two public relations firms were devising a strategy to respond to OCAW's campaign, the union acted to undermine the company's efforts.

The Kamber Group was well known by OCAW leaders. The firm's founder, Victor Kamber, had built the company into a "powerhouse" among public relations firms mostly by representing union clients. The Kamber Group itself was unionized and advertised this fact in its solicitations for union business. Kamber is credited with bringing public relations strategies to union battles when the "corporate campaign" was in its infancy,[20] and over the years represented such clients as the Airline Pilots Association, the AFL-CIO's Building and Construction Trades Department, The International Brotherhood of Teamsters, the United Food and Commercial Workers, and the United Brotherhood of Carpenters and Joiners, among other large and influential unions.

OCAW-IU president Joseph Misbrenner wrote an angry letter to Kamber and strongly objected to his association with AHP. Misbrenner accused him of "working both sides of the street" and sent copies of his letter to some of organized labor's top leaders (and some of Kamber's biggest clients) including Lane Kirkland, president of the AFL-CIO; Robert Georgine, president of the Building and Construction Trades Department; Robert Harbrant, president of the Food and Allied Service Trades Department; and Howard Samuel, president of the Industrial Union Department. Later, when OCAW obtained further documentation of Kamber's involvement through the RICO discovery, the union worked to publicize Kamber's involvement with AHP's campaign against the union and before long lengthy articles which characterized Kamber as duplicitous and unethical appeared in several national publications.[21]

Although there is plenty of evidence to show that AHP spent a substantial amount of money for Kamber's and Benchmarketing's advice, in the end the PR firms' strategy proved to be more smoke than fire. The campaign stalled before it really got underway and AHP attempted only one significant public relations remedy.

Kamber's evaluation of the Whitehall plant closing battle led it to the conclusion that "the dispute between American Home Products Corporation and the Oil, Chemical, and Atomic Workers International Union [was] due primarily to a serious breakdown in communications between the parties."[22] (Perhaps only a public relations firm could view the dispute in these terms.) Nevertheless, with an eye toward "improving communications," in April 1991, AHP issued "An Open Letter to the Community" in which it sought to "correct the record" and address the "many articles [that] included information which was erroneous." The company sent the letter to each Whitehall employee and published the letter as a full page advertisement in local newspapers.[23]

The letter said unequivocally that nothing the union did would cause the Whitehall plant to remain open, "we do not know why the union still believes we will reconsider our decision to close the Elkhart plant, because we will not do so...our decision to close the plant is final and irrevocable." The letter explained that the reason for the closure was over capacity due to the 1989 acquisition of another medical products company, A.H. Robins. It said that only eight percent of current production was being transferred to Puerto Rico and this would yield the company tax savings of just $500,000 annually. The remaining production would move to Hammonton, New Jersey and Richmond, Virginia.

The letter also pointed out that the company had tried to be amicable and responsible by giving union members an "almost unprecedented" 13 month advance notification of the closure and by the gift of the plant and land to the city. It offered to terminate any laid-off employees who wished it so they could receive their contractually mandated severance benefits immediately rather than wait for the plant to close six months later.

The company's letter initially had the desired effect. Many union members were frightened by the finality of the company's position and by its admonition, "let there be no mistake. . . . We are not going to be intimidated by these attacks . . . and we will fight each lawsuit and each unfair labor practice charge in the appropriate forum." AHP's message was clear; to fight was pointless because Whitehall would close on schedule and the company would prevail against the union's lawsuits. This was a compelling argument and it threatened the relatively solid base of support among Local 7-515 members for the union's campaign. As such, it also proved to be a momentous test of Malloy's leadership.

Union members had been essential to the progress of the campaign to this point. They did the work of the campaign; they mailed thousands of letters, prepared materials for the parade and rallies, administered a union food bank, emergency relief fund and job club, and collected and disseminated information about the campaign inside the plant. Also, they turned out in significant numbers for every press conference. This broad and public membership support, for the most part, precluded accusations from the press that the campaign was run by Denver-based international union "outsiders." As a result, news accounts focused mainly on the issues rather than on internal union politics. This focus was essential to the viability of the media campaign. Furthermore, membership solidarity was the foundation of the legal initiatives. The OCAW-IU could hardly be expected to continue to invest money and resources in lawsuits against the company if the Whitehall members decided to give up the fight.

AHP's letter shook the confidence and resolve of many members and caused underlying doubts about the campaign to surface. For days afterward, Malloy met and talked endlessly with members to try to answer their concerns and fears. She pointed out that if the company was intent on closing, then Whitehall workers had little to lose by a fight. She also enumerated the legal initiatives that could pay off financially and explained that to ". . . voluntarily elect to terminate their employment with Whitehall and receive their severance allowance" (as AHP's letter suggested) at this point would preclude them from receiving any settlements from the lawsuits. Also, when Whitehall employees were "laid-off," they still received medical insurance and accumulated seniority. Employees would give this up if they took their severance allowance and their medical insurance coverage would end in four months. She also argued that the company must be concerned about the union's campaign for it to go to the trouble of "correcting the record" with this letter and advertisement. In short, Malloy convinced members they had little to lose and a lot to gain by continuing to fight. In the end, no members elected to receive early severance pay and membership support remained as solid as it ever was.

The union retained membership support throughout the many months of the campaign because it pursued tangible avenues of redress. In so doing, it mitigated the risks of the fight. Not only could Malloy argue for solidarity and perseverance on moral grounds, she could point to the possibility of real financial benefits. "Workers of Whitehall Unite" simply would not have been as persuasive as was the possibility of a treble damages award in the RICO suit or back pay awards in the WARN or NLRB cases. This is not to suggest that the workers' only motivation was monetary payoff. They knew a settlement of any kind was, at best, months off and perhaps years. The point is that when doubts arose and they wondered whether the fight was worth the trouble and uncertainty, Whitehall workers had more than one good reason to stay with it.

Benchmarketing and Kamber planned for this letter to be the first of a series which would be sent to employees and the community until the plant closed in November. However, no other such communications were dispatched. The PR firms made several other suggestions which AHP declined to implement. In fact AHP seemed to ignore many of the more aggressive tactics the firms suggested. For example, in May 1991, the union failed to attend a scheduled meeting with the NLRB at which the union and the company were to continue their discussions to try to settle the NLRB claims before the issues were brought to trial. The PR firms wanted to exploit this opportunity and cast the union as obstructionist and unwilling to negotiate with the company. In one draft of a letter, the firms would have had AHP point out that the "company was prepared at those meetings to increase substantially the termination benefits [employees] will receive, but [could] not do so now." AHP probably guessed that this type of statement would inflame OCAW and compel the union to file an additional unfair labor practice charge for circumventing union leadership. Subsequent drafts played down and finally deleted all references to AHP's willingness to have increased severance benefits. Yet, ultimately, no letter regarding OCAW's withdrawal from the NLRB negotiations ever was sent.

Concern about a union counterattack probably tempered AHP's PR response throughout the campaign but especially in the spring of 1991 when OCAW's legal actions were underway and showing promise. OCAW had demonstrated unequivocally that it would pounce on every PR opportunity that presented itself. Still, "arrogance" and its desire for "anonymity" seemed to color AHP's response as much as fear of union reprisal did. For AHP, the PR campaign was simply an unpleasant exercise, one to which it neither committed nor attached much importance.

AHP's skepticism about the value of an aggressive PR campaign probably reflected its general aversion to corporate PR. The absurdity of Kamber's campaign assumption (that the dispute could be attributed to a "serious breakdown in communications") undoubtedly lent credence to this skepticism. Also, the plant was due to close in a few months and AHP managers probably figured they could weather any further negative publicity until then.

Perhaps the best explanation for AHP's confidence (or arrogance, as the union preferred to characterize it) lay in a faith in its ability to deflect the union's legal initiatives and prevail in the courtroom. Beyond its half-hearted PR effort, the company contained its fight to judicial venues in which it was reasonable to presume that the union was at a disadvantage. AHP's strategy made sense; all it would take to derail the campaign was a favorable ruling on one of the company's many motions against the RICO suit. This would have undercut the union's leverage significantly and could have forced a quick return to the effects bargaining table. It seems unlikely that AHP could have predicted the impact of Puerto Rican politics on the progress of the RICO suit. Thus, the company chose the most logical course of action.

AHP tried little else in the way of public relations in the remaining months before the shutdown and its final attempt was characteristically ill-timed and ultimately counterproductive. The plant closure was set for November 1 and OCAW decided to stage a demonstration on Halloween, the eve of the closure. The union arranged for a theater troupe from Chicago to entertain the workers and asked everyone to come dressed in Halloween costumes. Whitehall officials, who apparently concluded that this was a farewell get-together, arranged to provide refreshments and portable latrines for the event. Little did the company know that the theater troupe would parody AHP chairman Stafford and other AHP executives and that NBC News would be there to film the event for a story on plant closings. Thus, instead of gaining favor among exiting employees, AHP unwittingly played into the union's lampoon and opened itself up to further derision and scorn from the workers.

Labor-Management Relations. A more aggressive PR campaign not only would have been illogical, it also would have been inconsistent with AHP's labor relations style and reputation. One of the more ironic features of this plant closing battle was that AHP was the target. In the years preceding the Whitehall campaign, AHP's labor policies were considered by many high-level organized labor leaders to be exemplary and representative of the way companies ought to treat labor unions. These labor leaders credit AHP's senior vice-president for industrial relations, Joseph Bock, with establishing the amiable tone of labor-management relations between the company and the unions that represented AHP workers. OCAW too had enjoyed a friendly relationship with Bock and believed AHP "treated [OCAW] members fairly," and said so in a 1985 endorsement in its bi-monthly publication, *OCAW Reporter*.[24]

Leaders of the Industrial Union Department (IUD) of the AFL-CIO, in particular, admired Bock's labor policies and practices. They viewed Bock as a skilled negotiator who invariably treated unions honorably and with respect. In 1989 for example, they called on Bock to help settle a long and contentious strike by 40,000 Communications Workers of America (CWA) and 20,000 members of the International Brotherhood of Electrical Workers (IBEW) against NYNEX Corporation, a "Baby Bell" telephone company that services the New York and New England areas. The IUD even gave Bock a rare medal, which was a souvenir from the 1955 AFL-CIO merger, to "celebrate [his] invaluable help in settling the NYNEX strike."[25] Bock and other AHP managers were frequently invited to attend the IUD's annual meetings and Bock occasionally was a featured speaker at the meetings.

Also, the United Food and Commercial Workers (UFCW) union called AHP "tops in labor relations" in a 1984 edition of its bimonthly publication, *UFCW Action*. "American Home Products is an outstanding company," said UFCW president William Wynn in the same article, "its corporate management is a model I wish more companies would follow, because I believe that honest and fair labor-management relations go hand-in-hand with profits."[26]

This respect and admiration for AHP and particularly Bock was an obstacle to OCAW's campaign because it precluded a united labor front on the issue of Section 936-inspired runaways, at least until the company settled with the union. Some suggest that even after the settlement, Bock's alliances continued to have an impact on the intensity of the commitment by organized labor to reform Section 936. AHP attributes OCAW's failure to garner unmitigated support from organized labor to the union's reputation as an activist renegade that is out of step with mainstream labor. A combination of these reasons appears to be most explanatory.

Almost a year after the settlement, the new president of the AFL-CIO's Industrial Union Department sent a letter to the U.S. Secretary of Labor Robert Reich that praised a speech Bock made to the IUD-AHP coordinated bargaining committee. "I believe you will agree after you read the speech that the relationship between management and labor at AHP is a model to be replicated at every workplace," wrote Elmer Chatak.[27] This letter was sent just as the Section 936 hearings commenced in the House. While it does not specifically mention Section 936 or AHP's connection to the debate, it does illustrate a persistence of support for Bock and AHP that would suggest ambivalence toward OCAW's efforts by some organized labor leaders.

As for AHP's opinion that OCAW is a fringe union, the union proudly wears its activist reputation on its sleeve and admits that on some issues it is out of step with mainstream organized labor. For example, OCAW was one of a few unions to break with the AFL-CIO position and oppose the Vietnam War, it was the first to file a complaint under the Occupational Health and Safety Act in 1971, and it was in the minority in the AFL-CIO Executive Council in voting against support of the anti-ballistic missile and the B-1 bomber in the 1970's.[28] More recently, OCAW was one of only a handful of labor unions in 1994 to oppose the AFL-CIO's support of a "managed care" system for health care reform.[29] (The OCAW advocates a single payer, Canadian-style system.) Also, OCAW has been at the forefront of discussions about the formation of a third political party through its support of the Labor Party Advocates.[30]

Clearly, both Bock's favor in the labor community and OCAW's willingness to act independently of the AFL-CIO created obstacles to OCAW's campaign, especially before but also after the settlement.

CONCLUSION

Precedence and Enhanced Expectations

This union fight stands out because it had extraordinary national ramifications and it resulted in significant financial benefits for its members. The union used non-traditional resistance strategies which proved to be remarkably effective in bringing attention to its struggle and to the issues that motivated it. In a larger sense, the union's sophisticated media campaign and its pursuit of legal and legislative remedies for what it viewed as injustices serve as a model of contemporary American activism. This case shows how institutional and political change is effected today.

Yet it is not simply the union's resistance tactics which set this struggle apart. Very few of the *strategies* the union tried were unprecedented. Malloy, for example, drew on the experiences and union fights she read about in her university labor studies courses and consulted with local labor advocates for ideas on how to prevent the Whitehall closure. Similarly, LeRoy knew from his years of experience at the MCLR which shutdown resistance tactics might work and in fact, had written a book on how workers could predict and prevent a plant closure.[31] Leonard is one of the country's most successful corporate campaign strategists, and his experiences in other campaigns served as the foundation of the Whitehall effort. The relevance of this campaign is not that its tactics were entirely novel or unprecedented but that in some very important and historic ways, it succeeded.

A successful union campaign is itself an anomaly and as such may serve as a model for other unionists who struggle to find ways to prevail in disputes with employers. OCAW's activism currently is viewed by some as radical, but to the extent that its methods are adopted by other unions, the OCAW model may become the rule rather than the exception. The simple fact of OCAW's success in the Whitehall campaign and runaway plant reform effort may create enhanced expectations among other unionists. As with any union gain, this could manifest in tougher union collective bargaining positions, higher severance benefit demands in shutdown situations, and generally a higher opinion of unions among workers. Knauss has reported that this seems to be the case in northern Indiana where the OCAW campaign is well-known.[32]

Power and the Powerless

This struggle—the issues, the players, the strategies, and the outcome—reveals the current state of power and politics in the United States. In particular, it demonstrates one way in which the relatively powerless can impel institutional action to their benefit, that is, by compelling those with power to act on their behalf. OCAW invoked the power of the courts, the power of Congress, the power of political influence in Puerto Rico, and the power of angry American taxpayers to its cause and brought about an unprecedented financial settlement and significant federal tax law reform. Yet, the plant closed, which suggests there are limits to this strategy, and the union got less than it set out for financially and legislatively, which suggests there are risks, too.

The biggest risk relatively powerless groups face when they form alliances with powerful institutions and individuals is that at some point common interests may become secondary to divergent ones. Few of OCAW's powerful allies were concerned only with the welfare of the workers at Whitehall. The union's allies in Congress were at least as concerned with the federal budget deficit and inefficient tax subsidies as they were with runaways or job loss in Elkhart, Indiana. The union's allies in Puerto Rico cared because OCAW's resistance to the closure and to Section 936 served their own political agendas, namely the statehood and independence movements. OCAW's allies in the American taxpaying electorate were as concerned about the level of taxation as they were with the fairness of how their taxes were spent. Even OCAW's RICO attorneys, its courtroom allies, had competing financial interests intrinsic to contingency fee-based legal representation. What, for instance would the union's RICO attorneys have done had AHP agreed to keep open the plant? (Of course, AHP never did.) Would they have pushed for a settlement anyway?

Thus, when competing concerns could be met with measures that did not necessarily address the concerns of the union, the union's interests became secondary. For example, when the Congress realized it could raise revenues and correct tax inefficiencies with a cut in Section 936, OCAW's anti-runaway amendment became unimportant. Likewise when the Congress learned there might be a price to pay for a cut in Section 936 by way of increased welfare payments to Puerto Ricans formerly employed by Section 936 companies, the risk of taxpayer wrath at the polls was mitigated. And again, OCAW's goal to prevent further runaways was lost in the shuffle of competing political considerations. Similarly, as the Puerto Rico statehooders rode the momentum of the anti-Section 936 sentiment, their interest in OCAW's problems waned as their own naturally took precedence.

Of course, OCAW had no choice but to live with these risks since its only alternative was to accept its relative powerlessness and do little or nothing. Furthermore, these risks are only apparent in hindsight and pale when compared to other risks union members knowingly took along the way. The biggest of these was certainly the very real risk of ending up with less than what they started with, both financially and personally. This campaign was messy and expensive and many people on all sides suffered and continue to suffer tremendous personal and professional damage, not only because of the shutdown but also because of the battle itself. The price of the fight was high. Nevertheless, the price of no fight would have been higher.

The beauty and hope of the American system is that sometimes the ordinary everyman or woman wins. Such was the case here. Although political and special interest machinations may not seem democratic when they are employed by very powerful interest groups, this case study illustrates that even the relatively powerless, given the right moment in time, can invoke the power that does exist and use this system to their advantage. However, inasmuch as this case serves as a testament to the American system, it also should serve as a warning—that only the very smart, politically sophisticated, and unafraid will have a chance.

NOTES

[1]   Richard Leonard, interview by author, 25 February 1994.

[2]   Connie Malloy, interview by author, March 1995.

[3]   Paul Jarley and Cheryl Maranto, "Union Corporate Campaigns: An Assessment," *Industrial and Labor Relations Review,* 43 (July 1990):5, p. 519. Jarley and Maranto warn that estimates such as theirs which were obtained through public reports should be viewed with "considerable caution."

[4]   There were two OCAW local unions which represented workers at Whitehall Laboratories in Elkhart. Local 7-838 represented laboratory inspectors, line inspectors, and chemists. Local 7-838 split from Local 7-515 in 1972. According to Malloy, Local 7-838 members "viewed themselves as professionals and identified more with management than with the union." During the campaign to keep Whitehall open, Local 7-838 leaders refused to join Local 7-515 in their NLRB charges against the company and also refused to participate in the union's campaign activities. Individual members of Local 7-838 (usually about 7 people) did support Local 7-515's campaign but most of the volunteers during the campaign were members of Local 7-515. (Connie Malloy, "Taking On American Home Products: A Description and Analysis of the Fight to Keep Whitehall Open," (manuscript: Indiana University at South Bend, 1991), pp. 8.13-8.15.)

[5]   *Oil, Chemcial, and Atomic Workers International Union v. American Home Products Corporation,* 91-1093 and 92-1238. (Plaintiffs' Memorandum in Support of Final Approval of the Proposed Settlement, p. 10.)

[6]   Donald Stewart, former president and plant chairman of the ECWU at Wyeth, Ltd. in Windsor, Ontario, interview by author, 7 April 1994.

[7]   Bureau of National Affairs, *Basic Patterns in Union Contracts* (Washington, D.C.: BNA Books, 1992).

[8]   Formerly called the Industrial Cooperative Association, the organization is based in Boston, Massachusetts.

9   Todd Dickard, "Whitehall bars state-funded 'union' consultant," *Michiana Business Journal,* 30 November- 6 December 1990.

10 Greg LeRoy, correspondence to author, 2 April 1995.

11 U.S. General Accounting Office, *Multiple Employment Training Programs: Major Overhaul Needed to Create a More Efficient, Customer-Driven System* (Washington, D.C.: GAO/T-HEHS-95-70, February 1995), p. 1.

12 Ibid., pp. 1-7.

13 Doreen Hemlock, "Pharmaceuticals to bear bulk of new taxes," *San Juan Star,* 25 August 1993.

14 Milt Freudenheim, "American Home enters limelight," *New York Times,* 15 February 1988; *Hoover's Handbook of American Business, 1994;* Milton Moskowitz, Robert Levering and Michael Katz, *Everybody's Business: A Field Guide to the 400 Leading Companies in America* (New York: Doubleday, 1990), p. 172.

15 AHP hired John Skule, formerly of Bristol-Myers Squibb, as vice president for corporate affairs. He left AHP in late 1993.

16 Jeff Kurowski, reporter for the *South Bend Tribune,* interview by author, 23 May 1994; Jim Miller, reporter for the *Elkhart Truth,* interview by author, 27 May 1994.

17 The idea for the facility donation actually was proposed to the Elkhart city administration by the union in a package of "community severance" ideas.

18 Jim Miller, "Higher profile," *Elkhart Truth,* 15 February 1991.

19 Oil, Chemical, and Atomic Workers International Union, Press Conference, "Press Registration List, " (Washington, D.C.: National Press Club), 22 January 1991.

20 James Warren, "Ambition," *Regardie's,* 1987.

21 Jonathan Tasini, "Both Sides Now: Can a Labor Consultant Help Defeat a Union? Victor Kamber Has." *Village Voice,* 11 August 1992, pp. 39-40; Naftali Bendavid, "Kamber Group to Boss: Which Side Are You On?" *Legal Times,* 19 July 1993; Merrill Goozner, "PR firm draws fire in plant-closing fight," *Chicago Tribune,* 21 April 1991.

22 Victor Kamber and John Leslie to Joseph Bock, memorandum, 12 March 1991.

23 "An Open Letter to the Community," advertisement, *Elkhart Truth,* 8 April 1991; "An Open Letter to the Community," advertisement, *South Bend Tribune,* 8 April 1991.

24 "Buy these union-made products," *OCAW Reporter,* 40 (January-February 1985):11-12, p. 10.

25 Howard Samuel, (president, Industrial Union Department, AFL-CIO), to Joseph Bock (vice-president, American Home Products), letter, 14 November 1989.

26 "Top company in profits tops in labor relations," *UFCW Action,* July-August 1984, pp. 6-7.

27 Elmer Chatak (president, Industrial Union Department, AFL-CIO) to Robert Reich, (U.S. Secretary of Labor), letter, 13 March 1993.

28 Ray Davidson, *Challenging the Giants: A History of the Oil Chemical and Atomic Workers International Union* (Denver, Colo.: Oil, Chemical and Atomic Workers Union, 1988), chapter 42.

29 Laura McClure, "Labor and healthcare reform," *Z Magazine,* January 1994, p. 52.

30 William Greider, "Down but not out: Labor struggles to find its voice," *Rolling Stone Magazine,* 17 October 1991, p. 40.

31 Greg LeRoy, Dan Swinney, and Elaine Charpentier, *Early Warning Manual Against Plant Closings* (Chicago: Midwest Center for Labor Research, 1988).

32 Keith Knauss, interview by author, 20 March 1995.

Bibliography

Books

Aaron, Henry J. and Michael J. Boskin, eds. *The Economics of Taxation.* Washington, D.C.: The Brookings Institution, 1980.

Barlett, Donald and James Steele. *America: What Went Wrong?* Kansas City, Mo.: Andrews & McMeel, 1991.

Barone, Michael and Grant Ujifusa. *The Almanac of American Politics.* Washington, D.C.: National Journal, Inc., Times-Mirror Company, 1994.

Bloomfield, Richard J., ed. *Puerto Rico: The Search for a National Policy.* Boulder, Colo.: Westview Press, Inc., 1985.

Brody, David. *Workers in Industrial America: Essays on the Twentieth Century Struggle.* New York: Oxford University Press, 1980.

Bureau of National Affairs, Inc. *Basic Patterns in Union Contracts.* Washington, D.C.: BNA Books, 1989.

_____. *Basic Patterns in Union Contracts.* Washington, D.C.: BNA Books, 1992.

Carr, Raymond. *Puerto Rico: A Colonial Experiment.* New York: New York Univ. Press, 1984.

Clark, Gordon L. *Unions and Communities Under Siege: American Communities and the Crisis of Organized Labor.* New York: Cambridge Univ. Press, 1989.

Corry, John. *TV News and the Dominant Culture.* Washington, D.C.: Media Institute, 1986.

Craypo, Charles and Bruce Nissen, eds. *Grand Designs: The Impact of Corporate Strategies on Workers, Unions, and Communities.* Ithaca, New York: ILR Press, 1993.

Davidson, Ray. *Challenging the Giants: A History of the Oil, Chemical, and Atomic Workers International Union.* Denver, Colo.: Oil, Chemical, and Atomic Workers Union, 1988.

Dietz, James. *Economic History of Puerto Rico: Institutional Change and Capitalist Development.* Princeton, N.J.: Princeton Univ. Press, 1986.

_____. and Emilio Pantojas-García. *Colonial Dilemma: Critical Perspectives on Contemporary Puerto Rico.* Boston: South End Press, 1993.

Goldfield, Michael. *The Decline of Organized Labor in the United States.* Chicago: University of Chicago Press, 1987.

Heckscher, Charles C. *The New Unionism: Employee Involvement in the Changing Corporation.* New York: Basic Books, 1988.

Herman, Edward S. and Noam Chomsky. *Manufacturing Consent: The Political Economy of the Mass Media.* New York: Pantheon Books, 1988.

Hoover's Handbook of American Business, 1994.

Kochan, Thomas, Harry C. Katz, and Robert B. McKersie. *The Transformation of American Industrial Relations.* New York: Basic Books, 1986.

Mann, Eric. *Taking on General Motors: A Case Study of the UAW Campaign to Keep GM Van Nuys Open.* Los Angeles: Institute of Industrial Relations, Univ. of California, 1987.

Marshall, Ray. *Unheard Voices: Labor and Economic Policy in a Competitive World.* New York: Basic Books, 1987.

Meléndez, Edgardo. *Puerto Rico's Statehood Movement.* Westport, Conn.: Greenwood Press, Inc., 1988.

Mishel, Lawrence R. and Paula Voos, eds. *Unions and Economic Competitiveness.* Armonk, New York: M.E. Sharpe, 1992.

Moskowitz, Milton, Robert Levering, and Michael Katz. *Everybody's Business: A Field Guide to the 400 Leading Companies in America.* New York: Doubleday, 1990.

Nissen, Bruce, ed. *U.S. Labor Relations, 1945-1989: Accommodation and Conflict.* New York: Garland Publishing, 1990.

Perruci, Carolyn C., et al. *Plant Closings: International Context and Social Costs.* New York: Aldine de Gruyter, 1988.

Perry, Charles. *Union Corporate Campaigns.* Philadelphia: Industrial Research Unit, The Wharton School, Univ. of Pennsylvania, 1987.

Portz, John. *The Politics of Plant Closings.* Lawrence, Kan.: University Press of Kansas, 1990.

Way, Harold E. and Carla Weiss, comps. *Plant Closings: A Selected Bibliography of Materials Published through 1985.* Ithaca, New York: Martin P Catherwood Library, NYSSILR, Cornell Univ., 1987.

Weiss, Carla, comp. *Plant Closings: A Selected Bibliography.* Ithaca, New York: Martin P. Catherwood Library, NYSSILR, Cornell Univ., 1991.

Government Documents

Clinton, William J. *Vision of Change for America.* Washington, D.C.: GPO, 17 February 1993.

Congressional Budget Office, *Reducing the Deficit: Spending and Revenue Options.* A Report to the Senate and House Committees on the Budget, Washington, D.C.: GPO, February 1993.

Congressional Budget Office. *Industrial Policy Debate.* Washington, D.C.: GPO, December 1983.

Congressional Budget Office. *Potential Economic Impacts of Changes in Puerto Rico's Status Under S. 712.* Washington, D.C.: GPO, April 1990.

Joint Committee on Taxation. *General Explanation of the Revenue Provisions of the Tax Equity and Fiscal Responsibility Act of 1982.* Washington, D.C., December 1982.

U.S. Congress. House. Committee on Government Operations. Employment and Housing Subcommittee. *Waste and Misuse of Federal On-the-Job Training Funds.* 102nd Cong., 2d sess., 5 August 1992.

U.S. Congress. House. Committee on Ways and Means. *President Clinton's Proposals for Public Investment and Deficit Reduction.* 103rd Cong., 1st sess., 1 April 1993.

U.S. Congress. Senate. Committee on Finance. *Administration's Tax Proposals (Foreign Tax and the Possessions Tax Credit-Section 936 of the Internal Revenue Code).* 103rd Cong., 1st sess., 27 April 1993.

U.S. Department of Commerce, Bureau of the Census. *Statistical Abstracts of the United States.* Washington, D.C.: GPO, 1993.

U.S. Department of Labor, Bureau of Labor Statistics. *Employment and Earnings.* Washington, D.C.: GPO, August 1992.

_____. *Occupational Compensation Survey, Elkhart-Goshen, Indiana Metropolitan Area, October 1991.* Washington, D.C.: Bulletin 3060-62, August 1992.

U.S. Department of the Treasury. *Operation and Effect of the Possessions Corporation System of Taxation, Sixth Report.* Washington, D.C.: GPO, March 1989.

U.S. General Accounting Office. *Multiple Employment Training Programs: Major Overhaul Needed to Create a More Efficient, Customer-Driven System.* Washington, D.C.: GAO/T-HEHS-95-70, February 1995.

_____. *Pharmaceutical Industry: Tax Benefits of Operating in Puerto Rico.* Washington, D.C.: GAO/GGD-92-72BR, May 1992.

_____. *Tax Policy: Puerto Rico and the Section 936 Tax Credit.* Washington, D.C.: GAO/GGD-93-109, June 1993.

U.S. International Trade Commission. *Impact of the Caribbean Basin Economic Recovery Act on U.S. Industries and Consumers.* (Eighth Report-1992), Washington, D.C.: USITC Pub. 2675, September 1993.

Reports and Manuscripts

AFL-CIO. Industrial Union Department. *Developing New Tactics: Winning with Coordinated Corporate Campaigns.* Washington, D.C.:, Industrial Union Department, AFL-CIO, 1985.

American Home Products Corporation. *Annual Reports, 1988-1991.* Madison, N.J.: American Home Products Corp.

Commonwealth of Puerto Rico. Puerto Rico Economic Development Administration. "Highlights of the Drug and Pharmaceutical Industry in Puerto Rico." RCM9902.5/796, September 1990.

Investor Responsibility Research Center, Inc. "Plant Closings and Dislocated Workers: American Home Products Corp." Washington, D.C.: IRRC 1992 Background Report J, 31 March 1992.

LeRoy, Greg, Dan Swinney, and Elaine Charpentier. *Early Warning Manual Against Plant Closings.* Chicago: Midwest Center for Labor Research, 1988.

Malloy, Connie. "Taking on American Home Products: A Description and Analysis of the Fight to Keep Whitehall Open." manuscript, Indiana University at South Bend, 1991.

Midwest Center for Labor Research. "Jobs Exported to Puerto Rico." Chicago: Midwest Center for Labor Research, 17 June 1991.

_____. "Social Cost Analysis of Possible Shutdown of Whitehall Laboratories, Elkhart, Indiana." Chicago: Midwest Center for Labor Research, September 1990.

Oil, Chemical, and Atomic Workers Union, "OCAW Comparison and Analysis of Drug and Cosmetic Groups Selected Contract Provisions." Prepared by OCAW for the Drug and Cosmetic Council Meeting. Washington, D.C., 18-22 June 1989.

_____. "Agreement between Whitehall Laboratories, Inc. and Local 7-515, Oil Chemical, and Atomic Workers International Union, AFL-CIO." effective 15 September 1986.

Price Waterhouse. "Benefits and Costs of Section 936." Washington, D.C.: Prepared for Puerto Rico, U.S.A. Foundation, May 1991.

Puerto Rico Department of Labor and Human Resources. *Census of Manufacturing Industries of Puerto Rico.* 1990.

Articles

ABA Journal. "Toxic World of Allan Kanner." July 1989.

Bendavid, Naftali. "Kamber to Boss: Which Side Are You On?" *Legal Times,* 19 July 1993.

Bryan, Tom. "Union Rejects Runaway Plants Regulations." *Caribbean Business,* 12 March 1992.

Business Week."Rebel With a Cause, Actually, Several." 18 June 1990.

Chemical Marketing Reporter. "OCAW Hits Puerto Rico Move by AHP." 239 (28 January 1991):4.

Craypo, Charles. "Strike and Relocation in Meatpacking." In *Grand Designs: The Impact of Corporate Strategies on Workers, Unions, and Communities,* edited by Charles Craypo and Bruce Nissen. Ithaca, New York: ILR Press, 1993.

Datz, Harold, et al. "Economic Warfare in the 1980's Strikes, Lockouts, Boycotts, and Corporate Campaigns," *Industrial Relations Law Journal,* 9 (1987):1.

De la Torre, Beatriz. "Runaway Plant Panic." *Caribbean Business.* 11 March 1993.

_____. "U.S. Unions, P.R. Gov't Fight Over Runaways." *Caribbean Business.* 4 March 1993.

Economist, The. "Recession's Fellini." 17 November 1990.

Famadas, Nelson. "Section 936: Myths and Realities." In *Puerto Rico:The Search for a National Policy,* edited by Richard J. Bloomfield. Boulder, Colo.: Westview Press, Inc., 1985.

FDC Reports, Prescription and OTC Pharmaceuticals. "Rep. Stark's Sec. 936 Bill to Prevent Plant 'Runaways' to Puerto Rico." 53:24 Chevy Chase, Md.: FDC Reports, Inc., 17 June 1991.

Feldstein, Martin. "A Contribution to the Theory of Tax Expenditures: The Case of Charitable Giving." In *The Economics of Taxation,* edited by Henry J. Aaron and Michael J. Boskin. Washington, D.C.: The Brookings Institution, 1980.

Glastris, Paul. "Pain Relief." *U.S. News & World Report,* 1 July 1991.

Goff, John. "Flight Fright at American Home Products." *Corporate Finance,* December 1990.

Greider, William. "Down But Not Out: Labor Struggles to Find Its Voice." *Rolling Stone Magazine,* 17 October 1991.

Henry, Lawrence. "The Strange Case of Section 936." *CFO Magazine,* May 1991.

Jarley, Paul and Cheryl Maranto. "Union Corporate Campaigns: An Assessment." *Industrial and Labor Relations Review,* 43 (July 1990):5.

Kaufman, Nancy. "Do the TEFRA Amendments Go Too Far?" *Wisconsin Law Review,* 2 (1984):533.

Klein, Joe. "The Year of the Voter." *Newsweek,* Special Election Edition, November/December 1992.

Kosterlitz, Julie. "Jawboning With a Bite: Chairman of Special Committee on Aging, David Pryor, Attacks Pharmaceutical Industry." *National Journal,* 24 (23 May 1992):21.

McClure, Laura. "Labor and Healthcare Reform." *Z Magazine,* January 1994.

Merrill, Peter. "The Possessions Tax Credit and Puerto Rican Economic Development." In *Puerto Rico: Search for a National Policy,* edited by Richard J. Bloomfield. Boulder, Colo.: Westview Press, Inc., 1985.

Mytych-DelPonte, Anne. "Puerto Rico Tax Breaks Induce Firm to Relocate Jobs, Indiana Union Says." *Employment & Training Reporter,* 21 November 1990.

Nissen, Bruce. "A Post-World War II 'Social Accord?'" In *U.S. Labor Relations, 1945-1989: Accommodation and Conflict,* edited by Bruce Nissen. Garland Publishing, 1990.

O'Reilly, Brian, "Drugmakers Under Attack." *Fortune,* 29 July 1991.

Samborn, Randall. "Plant Shutdowns." *National Law Journal* 13 (29 July 1991):47.

Target Washington. "Chairman Miller Files Runaway Plant Bill." Washington, D.C.: Target Washington, 5 (16 April 1993):8.

_____. "Union Attacks Company on Move to P.R.." Washington, D.C.:Target Washington, 5 (8 January 1993):1.

_____. "Union Sues AHP for $1 Billion in Second Suit." Washington, D.C.: Target Washington, 4 (6 March 1992):5.

Tasini, Jonathan. "Both Sides Now: Can a Labor Consultant Help Defeat a Union? Victor Kamber Did." *Village Voice,* 11 August 1992.

Thompson, Ruth K. "Union Use of Public Proxy Resolutions." *Labor Studies Journal,* 13 (Fall 1988):3.

Trinidad, Pablo. "Storm Brewing Over Section 936?" *Caribbean Business,* 9 July 1992.

_____. "Acme Boot to Produce Footwear in Toa Alta." *Caribbean Business.* 10 December 1992.

_____. "Rallying the Forces: The Story Behind the Rescue of Section 936." *Caribbean Business,* 5 August 1993.

Newspapers

Chicago Tribune
Elkhart (Indiana) Truth
Michiana (SW Michigan/NC Indiana) Business Journal
New York Times
Press of Atlantic City (N.J.)

Newspapers (continued)
San Juan (Puerto Rico) Star
South Bend (Indiana) Tribune
Wall Street Journal
Washington Post
Wilmington (Delaware) News Journal

Index

DATE DUE